The Best Finish:
Adopting a
Retired Racing Greyhound

Carolyn Raeke

T.F.H. Publications
One TFH Plaza
Third and Union Avenues
Neptune City, NJ 07753
www.tfh.com

Distributed by T.F.H. Publications, Inc.

Book design by Candida Moreira Tómassini.

Library of Congress Cataloging-in-Publication Data
Raeke, Carolyn.
  The best finish : adopting a retired racing greyhound / Carolyn Raeke.
          p. cm.
      ISBN 0-7938-0535-X
      1. Racing greyhound.   2. Dog adoption. I. Title.

SF429.G8 R34   2004
636.753'4–dc22
2003016918

Table of Contents

Introduction:
From Kennel to Couch

She was born into a racing family, and those who knew her parentage had high hopes for her future. Her early months were spent in close companionship with her siblings, and she had plenty of exercise, running and racing with others in her group. Eventually she moved into her own crate, where she spent her time between exercise periods and training. She had frequent contact with people from the very beginning and was quite used to being touched and handled.

Her life was quickly regimented. When she was just a few months old, preparation for her racing career began with an exercise regimen of runs in various lengths. Then, at ten months, she started working with a drag lure, a mechanical device that drags an artificial lure along the ground where it is easily visible. Before she was two years old, she went to her first track, where she had to be among the top-four finishers within six maiden races to advance in racing grade. Although she did move up, she failed to win, place, or show in her first three races at the new grade. Having failed to live up to her expectations, at barely two years of age, she was taken away from the track and her hundreds of canine companions.

Racing Greyhounds spend their days in close companionship with each other. They exercise, race, eat, and sleep with other racers.

As she left the familiarity of the track and kennel, she was anxious. She was put inside another crate inside an unfamiliar vehicle, and soon she felt movement but didn't know what that meant. It helped that there were six others in the same vehicle, also in crates, and so she relaxed somewhat. When the van finally stopped, all of them were taken inside a building where they were given baths and had their nails trimmed, ears cleaned, and the ticks picked off their bodies and from between their toes. Then they were put into crates in that building and given a meal. Soon, exhausted after their long ride and the abrupt change in their lives, they lay quietly until, one by one, she and the others were taken out and put into separate vehicles with people they had never seen before.

A short time later, she was helped to climb a flight of stairs and she entered the living area of a house for the first time in her life. She didn't know it, but she was one of the lucky ones that day. The same year that she became a pet, tens of thousands of Greyhounds were destroyed because they didn't run fast enough and failed to make money for their owners.

Although she had had a racing name since she was three months old, it meant nothing to her. Now she was called Chloe, and she was a member of a new pack—a family.

Chloe soon discovered that instead of a wire crate with a bed of shredded newspaper that doubled as her only "toy," she had a fluffy dog bed or even the down-filled comforter on her new family's bed as a place where she could lie down. She had soft toys that she could toss into the air or cuddle up with. She was the center of attention at her new home, and everywhere she went people asked what kind of dog she was and where she came from. They all wanted to pet her and tell her how beautiful she was.

She flourished—the hair on her hindquarters grew back and her coarse coat became softer and shinier; her teeth sparkled from a professional cleaning and then regular brushing; she had toys to chew and a blanket to nest in. Life was good.

It was not that long ago that most people associated "Greyhound" with an interstate bus or perhaps a casual visit to a racetrack while vacationing in Florida. But since the late 1980s, the story of the ex-racing Greyhound has been chronicled in magazines, in newspapers, and on television news programs and documentary specials. Every day, more people recognize a Greyhound when they see him walking on a lead at someone's side, and they realize he was probably "rescued" from a track because his racing days were over.

Most of the thousands of Greyhounds now living as pets were once racing dogs who literally had to run for their lives. If they weren't fast enough, they faced two likely prospects: death (by humane means if they were lucky, but possibly by being left to starve, being clubbed over the head, or shot) or a new life as a pet.

Origin
and History

The Greyhound is one of the oldest breeds in existence and has been traced back thousands of years to early cave drawings. Greyhounds appear in literature, from the Old Testament of the Bible to the classic works of Ovid, Virgil, Chaucer, and Shakespeare. Greyhounds also appear in art in the works of the ancient Egyptians, the classical Greeks and Romans, and the medieval period. Greyhounds appear in 18th century British hunt scenes, in the works of 20th century artists like the fashion designer/illustrator Erte (who portrayed the Greyhound with sleek, stylish women), and even in contemporary advertising.

The Greyhound was the dog of pharaohs in ancient Egypt, of kings in ancient Greece, and of gentry and royalty in England. According to H. Edwards Clarke in *The Greyhound* (1965), "The dogs depicted on the tombs of long-dead pharaohs, on the mural friezes of Chaldean kings, on the vases and amphora of ancient Greece are proof enough that the Greyhound family was known to Arab peoples more than 4,000 years ago."

According to Roy Genders in *The Encyclopedia of Greyhound Racing: A Complete History of the Sport* (1981), a law of Canute in 1016 decreed "none but a gentleman," meaning a man of royal descent, was allowed to keep a Greyhound, and a Welsh proverb said: "you can tell a gentleman by his Greyhound and his hawk."

The Greyhound is one of the oldest, most regal breeds in existence. This breed was the dog of pharaohs in ancient Egypt, of kings in ancient Greece, and of gentry in England.

An illuminated manuscript in the British Museum, dating to the ninth century, depicts a chieftain and his huntsman with two Greyhounds. Kings Edward III

(1312–1377) and Charles II (1660–1685) had the Greyhound incorporated into their royal seals; King James I (1566-1625) was an avid fan of Greyhound coursing; and Queen Victoria's husband, Prince Albert, had a longhaired Greyhound, Eos.

Genders suggests several possible root words from which the name "Greyhound" could possibly be derived: the Anglo-Saxon *gre* or *grieg*, meaning "first in rank" of hounds, which later became *gradus*, meaning "first grade" or "most important;" the word *gaze*, referring to the dog's keen eyesight when hunting; or simply "grey" referring to the dog's soft gray eyes or soft gray coat. Apparently, the brindle color, which is one of the most prevalent among racing Greyhounds, was not introduced until the mid-18th century, when Lord Orford crossed the smooth-coated Greyhound with a Bulldog.

Originating in southern Arabia, the Greyhound was introduced into Egypt via incense caravans; then to Greece, possibly by Alexander the Great; then to the Roman world; and, finally, into Britain.

After Greyhounds were introduced into the US in the mid-1800s, primarily to rid mid-western farms of an epidemic of jackrabbits, they also were used by the US Cavalry to scout for and spot enemies because Greyhounds could keep up with their horses. General George Armstrong Custer reportedly traveled with a score of Greyhounds and was said to nap on a parlor floor in a sea of Greyhounds.

The Racing Greyhound

Coursing, in which these swift hounds chased down prey, was popular in ancient Egypt and Greece and later in the British Isles. It evolved from an open-field event to a race within an enclosed park with a dummy hare in 1876 in Hendon, England, and was refined into a hugely popular spectator sport (and gambling opportunity) in the US beginning in the 1920s after Owen Patrick Smith opened the first circular track in Tulsa, Oklahoma. A patent was taken out on a circular track and mechanical hare in 1890, but Smith was the first one to use it in an enclosed space.

Dog racing on a circular track with a mechanical lure actually evolved from coursing, in which swift dogs such as Greyhounds would chase down prey in an open field.

For more than 75 years in the US, the Greyhound's history has been dog racing's history, and it has been a story with many unhappy endings for many innocent Greyhounds.

Dog racing, which the industry says is the sixth-most popular spectator sport in the United States, has long been a sport with a high mortality rate. Some Greyhound adoption groups contend that as many as 25,000 Greyhounds who are retired from racing are still being killed each year, though racing proponents dispute that figure. Euthanasia is down to about 4,500-5,000 dogs per year, from about 12,000 in the mid-1990s, says Gary Guccione, executive director of the National Greyhound Association, the official registry for racing Greyhounds, and coordinator of the American Greyhound Council. The American Greyhound Council was founded in 1987 as a joint effort of the NGA and the track operators to protect the welfare of racing Greyhounds and to address industry humane issues.

According to the NGA, the annual number of Greyhound births—just over 34,000 in 2000—was reduced by 35 percent between 1990 and 2000. Twenty years ago in the United States, adopting an ex-racing Greyhound was virtually unheard of by most people, and racing opponents contend that the number of Greyhounds killed each year

Where is dog racing legal?

As of 2003, according to the American Greyhound Track Operators Association, there were 46 Greyhound tracks in the US, located in the 15 states where dog racing is legal: Alabama, Arizona, Arkansas, Colorado, Connecticut, Florida, Iowa, Kansas, Massachusetts, New Hampshire, Rhode Island, Texas, Oregon, Wisconsin and West Virginia. But Greyhounds are bred in 43 states, of which Kansas, Texas, Oklahoma, and Florida are the most prolific.

could well have been as many as 50,000. So many pups were born each year that Greyhounds who didn't make money at the track were a disposable commodity. There were always more of them coming up from the farms to take their racing kennel slots. Guccione says that at any one time there are some 37,000 Greyhounds "out there in the racing environment," referring to the Greyhounds on the active and inactive lists at the tracks and as puppies in the racing kennels.

A particularly sad aspect of Greyhound racing history is the use of these sweet, gentle dogs for medical research and the wanton destruction of them in inhumane ways. As recently as 2002, the owner of a dog farm in Alabama was reported to have shot and killed as many as 3,000 Greyhounds that he brought to his farm from the Pensacola Greyhound Track in Florida. Robert Rhodes told investigators he sometimes received ten dollars per dog and had been doing this for 40 years.

Two years earlier, Daniel P. Shonka, an NGA member who operated a racing kennel in St. Croix, Wisconsin and claimed to run an adoption group for retired racers out of his home in Iowa, was accused of illegally selling more than 1,000 dogs to a Minnesota medical research laboratory for $400 apiece. Shonka was a federally licensed dealer of

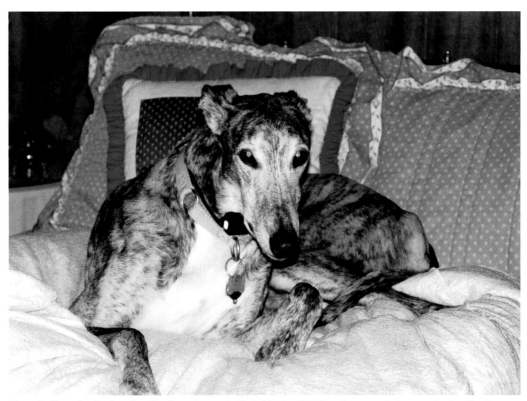

The adoption of retired racing Greyhounds was initiated in the 1980s, when people began placing the dogs into adoptive homes after they could no longer race.

animals for research. He was convicted in early 2003 of felony theft for taking the dogs without the consent of their owners and selling them for profit and was placed on probation for four years and fined $10,000. Shodan Enterprises, a corporation controlled by Shonka, pleaded no contest to six counts of felony theft and one count of felony theft by fraud and was fined $67,000. Wisconsin's attorney general said restitution, fines, and costs totaled more than $110,000.

Cynthia Cash of Baton Rouge, Louisiana, and Sherry Cotner, of North Carolina, a member of Greyhound Protection League, exposed Shonka's activities by following a paper trail made possible by filing Freedom of Information Act (FOIA) requests. They were able to obtain the ear tattoo numbers of Greyhounds and used those to contact the dogs' registered owners, who were unaware that their dogs had been sold to a research facility. "We know Greyhounds are the second-most preferred breed for research," after Beagles, says Cash, noting Greyhounds' docile nature, one of the qualities that makes them such wonderful pets, as well as their short coat, sleek body, long legs, ability to live in confines, and the heart and lung capacity of a small human. "So they are perfect for cardio and orthopedic research."

Because the experiments in which they were involved were terminal, only 98 Greyhounds could be rescued from the Minnesota research facility, but they all had to undergo surgery to reverse the cardiac pacemaker implants they had received—the facility required that, Cash says—and all but two, who died during the surgery, were put out for adoption through about 20 groups around the country. Both Shonka and Rhodes have been barred from Greyhound racing "and anyone doing business with them runs the risk of sanctions," says Guccione.

One legislative battle that is likely to continue in states with dog racing is the tracks' quest for video slot machine gambling to keep them financially viable. Economics will probably force some tracks to close because of increasing competition for the gambling dollar. Guccione acknowledges that interest in dog racing has diminished in recent years because of other forms of gambling, but he says the racing

With increasing numbers of retired racers being adopted each year, Greyhounds are quickly becoming one of America's most popular dogs.

purse has still increased from the mid-1990s, although that is partly because several tracks have slot machines to supplement the income.

The Racing Greyhound Adoption Movement

The history of retired racing Greyhound adoptions in the US really began in the early 1980s. The following is from a 1996 speech by Joan Belle Isle, president of The Greyhound Project, outlining the history of the US Greyhound adoption movement:

"The whole Greyhound adoption phenomenon in the US really started on two fronts in the early 1980s. There were always some breeders who made it their business to place their own dogs and I've seen some press clippings that actually show the Seabrook, New Hampshire, track adoption program to have been the first one in the country. The seminal development, however, occurred in Florida when Ron Walsek, who was then a pari-mutuel clerk at Derby Lane, began placing dogs through an organization he started and named REGAP.

The future of Greyhound adoption appears hopeful, and adoption groups across the country aim to be able to place all Greyhounds into homes after they retire from racing.

"The original REGAP group was primarily composed of people with ties to Greyhound racing…Many of the racing people who were originally attracted to the idea were what we would characterize as 'responsible' Greyhound people. They were not willing to accept that there was no future for their dogs when they could no longer race, and placing their dogs in adoptive homes was their way of taking responsibility for their own pups.

"From the stories I have heard, the early days in adoptions were not easy. Many of the breeders and trainers were not willing to give their dogs up for adoption."

However, the future of Greyhound adoption appears hopeful, with more and more retired racers being adopted every year. Guccione says: "About 90 percent of all the Greyhounds coming off the racetrack are adopted. Probably when you include all the puppies coming up that might not make it to the racetrack, 85 percent. We're still striving to get it to a hundred and the percentage does keep going up. We're working closely with especially the larger adoption groups, which is Greyhound Pets of America. They have a plan to get the extra four or five thousand adopted out by the year 2007, so we can have that basically at a hundred percent placement. They think it's doable and we think it is, too, and we're working with them."

Greyhound Pets of America was formed in 1987 after New England REGAP (Retired Greyhounds as Pets) invited various Greyhound adoption groups to join a national placement organization that would take a neutral position toward the racing industry. Some of the GPA's 42 chapters in 30 states even operate out of facilities at dog racing tracks. That first year, GPA placed 100 dogs. Six years later, it assisted in adoption of 3,188 Greyhounds, and in 2000, the number of adoptions was 4,347. What GPA calls its "7x7" program was started in 2002, with a goal of putting ex-racers into 7,000 "loving homes" annually by the year 2007.

For 7x7, GPA is using a volunteer "national Greyhound coordinator" to work with trainers, owners, and tracks that have tried to place dogs into local adoption programs that, for some reason, have been unable to take the dogs. The national coordinator's job is to find other groups that can take these dogs and also to arrange transportation. GPA says this effort should ensure "no one will have an excuse for not trying to get their unneeded Greyhounds into an adoption program."

Today there are hundreds of adoption groups and independent adoption efforts taking place worldwide. The NGA estimates that there are 240 adoption agencies

Hundreds of adoption groups and independent adoption efforts worldwide devote their time and resources to placing retired racing Greyhounds in loving homes.

devoted to retired racers in the US alone. The NGA also estimates that more than 150,000 Greyhounds have been adopted into homes as pets since 1990, and the current Greyhound population in the US and Canada exceeds 80,000, with 18,000 Greyhounds being adopted each year. Retired racing Greyhounds are quickly becoming one of America's most popular dogs.

Temperament
and Personality

*A*t one time, Greyhounds were thought to be unsuitable as pets because their training involved the use of live lures, mainly jackrabbits. But people who have adopted ex-racers know nothing could be further from the truth. Racing Greyhounds are not bred to be pets, but they take to pet life so naturally, you would think it is their reason for being.

Temperament

Considering the situation from which they have come—living with a huge pack of 60 to 80 other Greyhounds in a kennel that is one of ten such kennels at the track; moving from track to track, often in a downward spiral until they are finally at a facility with few or no resources for their care and maintenance; and then being turned over to the unfamiliarity of a whole new life with totally new people—Greyhounds are amazingly adaptable. They are also affectionate, easygoing, placid, gentle dogs who want to be loved. They like people and want to be where their people are, whether that is in the car, on the couch watching television, or in the bedroom sleeping. They are comfortable where you are. A Greyhound can stand, or preferably lie down, for hours at

Retired racing Greyhounds thrive on attention and love to be where their people are.

your side, a perfect testimonial to the Greyhound as a pet.

Some Greyhounds can be a little distant, but in general these are dogs that thrive on attention. Some are so demanding they will walk up and thrust a needle-nose into your armpit in a bid to be noticed. It is not unusual for a Greyhound who sees someone

One way to help your Greyhound overcome separation anxiety is to teach him that you will always return, so he won't fear being abandoned.

coming toward him to begin prancing and wagging his tail, if not his entire body, all in the expectation that the person will stop to visit. If he or she doesn't, you can almost tell by looking at him that the Greyhound can't understand why.

Shy Greyhounds will need time and patience to emerge from their shells. Their approach will be cautious, but over time the reticence will diminish as these shy dogs grow accustomed to their new homes.

Adjusting to Pet Life

Greyhounds are amazingly adaptable. They are also affectionate, easygoing, placid, gentle dogs who want to be loved. They like people and want to be where their people are.

Greyhounds' training allows them to develop strategy and think for themselves during a race. So even though initially you might find yours constantly on your heels and at your side, they can and do become independent. Some Greyhounds, however, bond too tightly to their adopters and can suffer from separation anxiety when left alone. This can lead to destructive behavior and much frustration for the adoptive family.

One way to help a Greyhound get over separation anxiety is to teach him that you will always return—after all, what he fears is being abandoned. If you discover that your Greyhound is destructive while you are out, start this teaching program. The first time, leave just long enough to step outside the front door, pause and then go back inside. Do this frequently for several days for differing lengths of time, but always for fairly short periods at the start. Whenever you have to leave your Greyhound behind, don't make a big deal of your departure. Dogs pick up cues like your putting on a coat or picking up the keys, and this triggers their anxiety. Do those things at times when you are not leaving, so your Greyhound doesn't just associate those activities with being left behind.

Greyhounds and Children

Many Greyhounds get along wonderfully well with children, and children should not be afraid of Greyhounds. But children must understand that while a Greyhound looks very different from most other breeds, he is still a dog and can respond as one in most situations. Children should always approach a Greyhound quietly and gently, and interactions between children and Greyhounds should be monitored by an adult. Parents are well advised to teach their youngster always to ask an owner's permission before petting a Greyhound, or any unfamiliar dog, especially since an ex-racer newly off the track may be shy or nervous and not welcome the petting.

Most Greyhounds are kind and gentle and get along wonderfully with children, but adults should always supervise their interactions.

Good relations between Greyhounds and children are largely dependent on what the child does or does not do, and that is the responsibility of the parent. Some children are too young to know how to act around a dog. Just because Greyhounds are widely known as gentle and passive doesn't mean that they will put up with being poked or pounded on or having their ears or tail pulled. Children should be taught specifically to respect a Greyhound's space at meal times and while he is sleeping, because a Greyhound who is eating may feel possessive about his food, and a sleeping Greyhound is easily startled. In either case, the Greyhound could, like many other breeds, react aggressively. If you use a crate, don't let the child go into it even if the Greyhound is not inside; that is your Greyhound's sanctuary, not a playhouse. Don't let children engage in rough play and tugging on toys with Greyhounds, who can become overly excited or even aggressive and thus accidentally injure a child.

Just Resting

In truth, Greyhounds spend the majority of their time in a prone position; if they aren't actually sleeping, they are resting. At the track, life consisted of a race that might last 30 seconds every two or three days, followed by lots of time lying around in a crate. Therefore, your ex-racer will spend a lot of time lying down — on his side; with his front legs straight out, his chest on the carpet or rug, and his haunches hovering (because of his large, muscular thighs) inches above that surface; or on his back with all four feet pointing toward the ceiling.

It is a common expression among Greyhound owners that their pet is a "45 mph couch potato." Bred and trained for speed, these dogs are incredibly fast. But once they leave the racing environment, they quickly run for the most comfortable place they can find. Greyhounds often will seek out your couch or your bed, so if you prefer your Greyhound on a dog bed or the floor, you will have to curb that inclination as soon as it appears, being insistent and consistent.

When you introduce your Greyhound to a child, be sure you have a good grip on his collar and pay attention to his body language. If he seems uneasy, keep him further away from the child. If possible, put a muzzle on your Greyhound as a precaution. Young children and Greyhounds happen to stand roughly eye-to-eye, which can be pretty scary for either of them. Greyhounds tend to see all the humans in their new home as part of their pack, and small children as young members of it. Smaller children should touch a Greyhound's side or back, very gently, rather than his face or head. Sudden movements or loud noises by excited or frightened children can, in turn, frighten a Greyhound into unpredictable behavior.

Greyhounds can be quite easy to walk on a lead, making it possible for older children to take on that responsibility. But these dogs are incredibly strong, so if your Greyhound pulls, it may be unwise to let any child hold the lead. If the child lets go and the Greyhound runs, you have one Greyhound lost and at risk of being injured.

Personality

Greyhounds can be very curious about their environment, especially when they first come from the racetrack and everything is new, but they are not busy in the way some other breeds are busy—constantly in motion, darting from room to room. A Greyhound's movements are more languid, with periodic bursts of energy.

There is a common misconception among those unfamiliar with ex-racers that Greyhounds are hyperactive. They are not. Ex-racers basically have two speeds: off and on. Their periodic bursts of activity, like the races they run, are of short duration. And then it is time to lie down again.

A Greyhound's sociability is readily apparent. Adoption groups that do public events with previously adopted Greyhounds regularly amaze people who stop to ask about the dogs. Half a dozen Greyhounds, many of them strangers to each other before that event, will be together in an exercise pen or just standing around attached to their people by leashes, with no snarling, growling, or snapping. Some Greyhounds will be standing to seek a friendly touch from visitors, while others might be lying down together, reclining on each other. And they won't be barking, either.

Greyhounds are generally quiet dogs. A hundred or more Greyhounds and their people can be indoors for a social event, and the only noise will be human conversation. Some ex-racers who go to homes where there are already barking dogs

Greyhounds are not hyperactive but actually spend most of their time lying down. Retired racers will often seek out your couch or bed in order to rest.

Thousands of Greyhounds get along well with cats and other pets, but supervise their introductions to make sure they are compatible.

may learn that behavior, but, in general, barking is confined to play behavior. They will make play bows—stretching out their front legs, dipping their heads, thrusting their hindquarters into the air—and maybe nip at the neck of a dog they are inviting to romp, emitting a sharp, rapid-fire series of barks. Such infrequent barking is a blessing for people who value quiet around the house, but it means most Greyhounds are not well suited to serve as watchdogs.

They can be enthusiastic greeters and are sometimes such vigorous tail-waggers that it is not uncommon for a Greyhound to break open the end of his tail by banging it forcefully against a wall, doorframe, or the sides of a crate.

Greyhounds like to play, although that may not manifest itself immediately after the dog arrives at his new home. At the track, they had no toys, and life was work. Once they discover the joys of throwing a stuffed animal into the air and pouncing on it or chewing on a soft toy to make it emit a squeak, they will return to those activities again and again. Squeak toys don't seem to last long with Greyhounds, who can puncture one with a tooth almost immediately. Some adopters buy extra squeakers by the dozens and spend hours installing them in toys to make them enticing once again.

For the most part, Greyhound play does not include "fetch" because these are not retrievers. Some Greyhounds will chase a ball, and even bring it back, and others will learn to catch a Frisbee®. On the other hand, their attitude frequently is: "You threw it, you get it. Oh, and bring it to me."

Greyhounds and Other Pets

The relationship between ex-racers' and cats is not always smooth. These are sighthounds, after all, bred and trained to chase something small that is moving, something humans might not even notice because it could be up to half a mile away. And that can just as easily describe a cat as an artificial lure. But just as Greyhounds show different degrees of competitiveness in a race, they show greater and lesser degrees of interest in and tolerance for small animals. Thousands of ex-racers do live with cats in peace and harmony, and many that initially showed a keen interest in a cat can be retrained over a period of time. But there are always some who cannot or will not be dissuaded from going after the cat. Needless to say, those Greyhounds should not live with one.

It is important to monitor the interaction of the Greyhound and any other animal, at least for some initial period, to avoid problems. Until you know your Greyhound well, put a muzzle on him when he is introduced to unfamiliar animals. Many Greyhounds do, however, get along well with other breeds of dog, with birds, and even, in some instances, with rabbits.

Greyhounds as Therapy Dogs

Many adopters take their Greyhounds to hospitals, especially those for children, and to nursing homes as therapy dogs. A hospital's requirements are usually the most stringent and often include a special orientation course, as well as certification and licensing by a recognized therapy dog organization, such as Therapy Dogs International. But many facilities for older citizens welcome Greyhounds without any special certification. Many adoption groups offer their own testing programs to ensure that particular Greyhounds are suited to making pet therapy visits. Those with shy or easily spooked Greyhounds should take advantage of such testing or otherwise expose those hounds to wheelchairs

Greyhounds are great therapy dogs because of their calm, easygoing nature, and many owners take their Greyhounds to hospitals and nursing homes for this purpose.

and walkers before visiting a nursing home or adult care residence; the sudden movement of these conveyances can be unsettling and startling to Greyhounds that have never seen them before.

Greyhounds do make very good pet therapy visitors. They are calm and easy-going. They are tall and thus easy to reach from a bed. They are long and thus present many areas for simultaneous petting. But they do tire and their attention wanders after about an hour, so visits longer than an hour are not recommended. Taking along some treats that residents or patients can give the Greyhound creates a bond between the human and the Greyhound. Greyhounds are surprisingly gentle in taking a treat from someone's hand, often to the delight of children and the amazement of adults.

Adopting an Ex-Racer

"Adoption ... a Greyhound's best finish." This mantra is popular among many people involved in Greyhound adoption. Their goal is to get retired racing Greyhounds across that finish line and into responsible, loving, permanent homes. But where do retired racing Greyhounds come from, and how can you find and adopt one?

Where To Adopt a Greyhound

Some of the adoption efforts started within the racing industry itself were aimed at countering criticism for the tens of thousands of perfectly healthy dogs it was destroying every year. Most adoption organizations are non-profit and volunteer-run, and many are completely independent of the racing industry. Still, they all must depend on people associated with racing as a source of dogs.

Greyhound rescue and adoption groups are listed in the phone directories in many areas, but if that doesn't work, try a local veterinarian, a humane shelter organization, or a pet store that invites Greyhound groups to bring in ex-racers so customers can learn what magnificent pets they are. Another option is to go on the Internet and perform a search for "Greyhound adoption." The list that pops up may be overwhelming, but just pick one. Almost any site you click on will have links to adoption groups.

The best way to obtain a retired racing Greyhound is to adopt one through one of the many non-profit rescue or adoption organizations that are active throughout the country.

If you see a Greyhound, talk to the person on the other end of that leash. Most people you see with a Greyhound would be happy to put you in touch with an adoption group.

Even if you live outside a particular group's placement area, that group should be able to direct you to a similar organization where you live.

Continuing negative publicity has prompted the racing industry to better its relations with the public at large and with adoption groups. The industry now lauds its own efforts on behalf of Greyhounds threatened by the seasonal and permanent closing of racetracks and by retirement.

If you see someone walking a Greyhound, talk to that person—he or she will probably be happy to recommend an adoption group for retired racers.

Nonetheless, there is an almost unlimited supply of Greyhounds available for adoption. Anyone active in coordinating rescue and adoption of Greyhounds can attest to the frequent calls they receive about hundreds of Greyhounds who suddenly become available because a particular track has closed for the season (or maybe even for good) or because dogs are not being moved to another track to continue racing.

Adoption Programs

At one track in the Eastern United States, the man who runs the adoption program through a Greyhound Pets of America chapter has helped put more than 3,000 retired racers into the hands of local adoption groups up and down the East Coast since 1996. With support from the track itself, he operates a holding kennel for Greyhounds that will not be continuing their racing careers and has fashioned a program that gets owners and trainers to help fund the transportation of ex-racers to adoption groups. The first year he moved 160 dogs into the adoption pipeline. The next year that number jumped to 500, where it has held steady ever since.

An individual adoption group may place only a hundred Greyhounds a year, with the number of dogs placed depending on how its adoption program is set up. Some groups can handle a larger number of dogs because they use kennels to house them, while others are limited by the availability of volunteers serving as foster homes.

Ex-racers may be placed in permanent homes directly from adoption group kennels, from foster homes where the dogs learn how to be house pets, or from a combination of initial kenneling and then home fostering.

Many retired racers are fostered and learn to become house pets before they are placed in permanent homes.

NGAP (National Greyhound Adoption Program) in Philadelphia, Pennsylvania, Greyhound Friends in Hopkinton, Massachusetts, and Operation Greyhound in San Diego, California, are among the adoption groups that maintain kennels for preparing ex-racers for adoption. NGAP, which also places dogs in areas far from its base in Philadelphia, started its program in 1989 and has full-time, live-in caretakers at its compound. The organization plans to build a new facility along the Delaware River with a capacity for 80 Greyhounds awaiting adoption and for another 80 Greyhounds and their friends who would be boarded.

Operation Greyhound, which has facilities for 23 Greyhounds at a time, places ex-racers primarily in Southern California and refers adoption inquiries from outside that area to the National Greyhound Adoption Network.

Greyhound Friends opened a new 4,000-square-foot kennel building in 2003. Greyhound Friends uses volunteers to help with chores at the kennel, including walking and socializing the retired racers. It also has a foster program to care for Greyhounds for from a few days to a few months, but primarily for short-term stays while the dogs recover from spay or neuter surgery. On its website, Greyhound Friends attaches a warning to prospective foster parents: "There is a shortage of foster parents because many of them adopt their wards!" Probably any rescue/adoption group that uses home fostering can issue a similar caveat.

TLC Greyhound Adoption was started in 1996 by sisters Deb Sanford and Sheryl Werner, who had a boarding kennel near Abilene, Kansas, in what they describe as "deep in the heart of Greyhound Country"—the state has two Greyhound racetracks and 400 Greyhound breeding farms and is home to the Greyhound Hall of Fame and the headquarters of the Greyhound racing industry.

TLC works with farm and kennel owners and operators in their area to find homes for Greyhounds, many of which have been sent back to the farms after being at tracks, but some of which have never raced. They send Greyhounds all over the country, to Canada, to other adoption groups, and to adopters who are attracted by their unusual fostering program, which just may put out for adoption some of the best-trained and socialized Greyhounds anywhere.

Inmate Fostering Programs

TLC Greyhound Adoption launched a very unique fostering program in January 2000, in cooperation with the state's Department of Corrections—the Kansas Correctional Facility Greyhound Project. A little over three years later, the program had "graduated" into adoptive homes 285 Greyhounds that had been fostered inside four correctional facilities in the state, according to Nancy Hudson, a nurse at one of the correctional facilities, coordinator of the fostering program, and also the instructor in obedience for the Greyhounds living with inmates.

"We have 34 dogs in prison right now," she says, which is the number of slots available for the fostering program. "We keep them filled. They remain with their inmates until they're adopted, and they're with the inmates 24/7."

The Ellsworth correctional facility made the initial overture, contacting founders Werner and Sanford and asking "for a couple of dogs as a trial program," Hudson says. "With all the budget cuts, they were cutting a lot of programs, and this program is free. It doesn't cost the state a penny. We're non-profit and we go off of our donations and grants and adoption fees. The state was eager to find a program that wouldn't cost anything and was open to this." Hudson says TLC's was the first such fostering program anywhere.

The program started in Ellsworth with two dogs and soon spread. In fact, it has spread outside Kansas, Hudson says, noting that TLC regularly fields inquiries from correctional facilities in other states and that there are 20 other such program around the country.

Hudson describes the prison fostering program as "win-win-win" and said she learned that "canine is the universal language" when she saw a Vietnamese inmate who spoke no English on his knees talking to a foster Greyhound, who was responding by wagging its tail.

"What is happy in a prison except a wagging tail?" she says. "There's nothing else happy about a prison. These dogs think prison is the most wonderful thing in the world. They come out of a cage somewhere, and a prison has flowers and grass" and a large fenced area where they can run.

Each Greyhound leaves the facility accompanied by a week-by-week journal kept by its handler or handlers. Hudson quoted from two journal entries:

Handler 1: "When I go to get her for break time (from his job), she gets all excited and even starts to whine a little. I feel like a parent going to daycare to get their child."

Handler 2: She "has a real stubborn streak in her. She wants to go where she wants to go. And if you don't want to go that way, she goes your direction sniffing the ground and tries to work around in a circle to the direction she wants to go, as if she's trying to trick you. I found the best way to deal with (her) is to be firm with her but let her get her way every once in a while. This keeps her confidence up so she doesn't feel or act defeated or depressed."

The inmate handlers cut toenails, clean teeth, groom, and give medications at weekly dog training classes. On its website—www.tlcgreyhoundadoption.com—TLC notes: "Most Greyhounds leave the program knowing how to walk nicely on lead, and the sit, down, stay, and come commands. Some are even superstars—DC, one of the first two dogs to enter the program, mastered an incredible 68 commands! Some of these Greyhounds are now therapy dogs, some live in group homes and care facilities, and some have gone on to just enjoy the life of spoiled family pets."

TLC does all its adoptions from the prison fostering program off its website, matching "people to dogs" based on a lengthy written application, Hudson explains. "People can't come see the dogs because they're in prison. People will drive hundreds of miles to pick them up. They want our dogs. They're housebroken, they're loving, and they're trained. They certainly have been loved. They've been gentled so much."

The success of the program is further demonstrated by the fact that some correctional employees who have come in contact with dogs at their facilities ask to adopt these foster Greyhounds.

The Adoption Process

All adoption groups have a variety of requirements, including written applications, visits to the homes of prospective adopters, and/or references from veterinarians or

Adoption groups place Greyhounds according to their compatibility with a family's existing members, particularly infants, toddlers, or other pets.

others who have adopted Greyhounds. They also generally require that someone adopting a Greyhound agrees to have the dog spayed or neutered, unless the organization has already done so before putting a dog out for adoption; to surrender the dog back to the organization in the event he can no longer be cared for; and not to use the animal for breeding, racing, or laboratory experiments. These tools help adoption groups place these deserving dogs with people who are eager to adopt a retired racer and who understand the special circumstances from which they come.

Some groups will let you pick out a dog, while others will "assign" you one based on his likely compatibility with your family makeup, particularly regarding infants, toddlers, cats, birds, and small dogs. You will have a choice of the sex of your dog and perhaps the color, although if you want a particular color, you may have a longer wait. Don't be upset if you can't just browse among a bunch of Greyhounds and pick out one you like. All ex-racers are wonderful—you won't be disappointed with the one you adopt.

Adopting A Senior Greyhound

One of the more recent developments benefiting ex-racing Greyhounds is a network that finds homes for Greyhounds aged seven years and older. Many of them come from breeding farms where they have outlived their usefulness to the racing industry, and others are Greyhounds previously adopted and suddenly displaced by a change in circumstance, such as the death of the person who adopted the dog. A prime mover in this senior Greyhound program is Kelly Graham of Cleveland, Ohio, who operates Golden Years Senior Greyhound Referral and has been finding homes for older Greyhounds since 1999.

Older retired racing Greyhounds make great companions for puppies, young dogs who are home alone, or dogs with separation anxiety.

Graham maintains websites—www.geocities.com/ohiogreyhounds/seniors and www.geocities.com/ohiogreyhounds/goldenyears—on which she posts information about senior Greyhounds in the US and Canada that need homes. Each listing has a color photograph of the Greyhound, along with a description of his personality and any special considerations for his placement, such as not being cat-friendly. She also posts information on available Greyhounds with special physical or emotional needs; there is no age minimum on these dogs.

"People ask how after living on a farm these dogs will act," Graham says of senior Greyhounds who have been used for breeding. "They'll act like a 60-pound couch potato."

Of senior Greyhounds in general, she says: "They are the most adaptable dog. A senior is so much more adaptable than a younger Greyhound. I've had dogs who walked into my living room, picked out a dog bed and parked on it, and it's like, 'I'm home.' All they want to do is be loved and love—and sleep and eat. These old dogs, they walk in and they're home."

Graham says a senior Greyhound makes an excellent companion for a younger, solo dog with separation anxiety. "They don't come any more mellow (than seniors)," she says.

Many adoption groups set up special funds to cover the costs associated with preparing older and injured Greyhounds for adoption and do not charge an adoption fee for a senior or special needs Greyhound. Those costs can be considerable, including surgery for broken legs in younger dogs, spaying or neutering older Greyhounds, and in their case, often extensive dental work, including the removal of many teeth.

Special Transportation for Adopted Greyhounds

Graham helps move senior Greyhounds to their new homes via the relay system dubbed the Greyhound Underground Railroad, or GUR. This is an example of how the Internet has truly revolutionized the rescue and adoption of Greyhounds. GUR is a time-intensive labor of love, so the system is not intended for transporting dogs that could be moved by another means. It is for dogs with no other reasonable way to get to a new home. Often the dogs have special needs—as with puppies, seniors, or Greyhounds with health or behavioral problems—and cannot be placed locally.

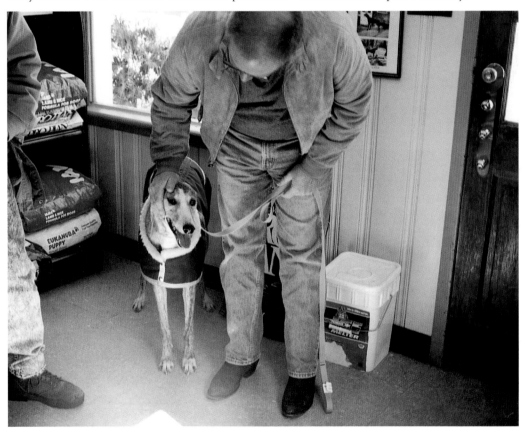

One unique method of transporting adopted Greyhounds is through the Greyhound Underground Railroad (GUR), where several volunteers transfer the dog through a relay system.

In preparation to transport the Greyhound, a GUR coordinator maps out one or more possible routes from starting point to destination and divides it into segments, usually from 50 to 150 miles long. Drivers for the segments are generally enlisted via the Internet. Sometimes the runs are as few as two or three segments, but other times a dozen or more transporters are involved. Each one hands the dog off to the next person until the Greyhound finally reaches its destination.

Many different individuals and groups use GUR and/or organize such trips. Runs, updated regularly until they are fully organized, appear on websites with detailed maps and charts showing each segment to be traveled, who will be driving, and noting which sections of the trip still need participants. Once everybody is in place, the trip for some lucky Greyhound gets underway. Later, photographs and the experiences of participants along the way may be sent back to the organizers for display on their websites.

Wings for Greyhounds is a non-profit organization, founded by pilot Maggie McCurry, which transports Greyhounds to adoption groups by airplane.

In addition to GUR, Greyhounds that are no longer of use to the racing industry are moved around the United States in private sedans and mini-vans, in trailers specially designed for transporting the dogs, and even by air.

Maggie McCurry took Greyhound adoption to new heights in 1996 when she started flying retired racing Greyhounds from racetracks in Arizona to groups in California and called it Wings for Greyhounds. A licensed pilot based in northern Arizona, McCurry describes her twin-engine airplane as a "flying mini-van." She took the middle row of seats out, "so the floor is just covered with blankets and pillows. I try to make it all nice and soft."

McCurry always flies with a co-pilot so she can concentrate on flying the plane and the co-pilot can "take care of the dogs." The kind of care that is taken

The Right Choice

All ex-racers are wonderful—you won't be disappointed with the one you adopt.

could make a commercial airline passenger jealous. "Somebody just delivers pets and TLC and blankies if they look too cold and a spray bottle if they look too warm. We do everything to try to keep them comfortable."

Although she has transported Greyhounds for medical emergencies, the hundreds of dogs she has flown are usually in groups of two to four retired racers going to adoption groups in states without racetracks. McCurry says that for it to be worthwhile for a hauler to get out the truck at the Tucson racetrack, he would need, for example, for California adoption groups to accept at least 28 dogs. Then he would have an 11-hour drive to Los Angeles, and more hours driving up the coast, dropping off a few dogs at a time to several groups. McCurry can fly to Los Angeles in two hours.

Tens of thousands of people have discovered how rewarding it is to adopt a retired racing Greyhound, and many have found that it's difficult to have just one.

Wings for Greyhounds is a media magnet and McCurry uses that "every bit I can. I can fly Greyhounds all day and all I've done is move a couple of Greyhounds. But if I can get a camera there, I can get dozens more adopted."

In 2002, she took that attention to a new level with the Great Greyhound Goodwill Tour, in which she flew 8,000 miles in 24 days, visiting 25 cities in 17 states and garnering local, and sometimes, national, newspaper and television coverage at each airport. The big attraction was that McCurry was either delivering two retired racing Greyhounds to an adoption group or picking up two to take to another group. The flying dogs were in the spotlight, and Greyhound adoption got an incredible boost.

Wings for Greyhounds is costly to operate and McCurry says, "We're always on the edge." She seeks grants and donations and sells T-shirts, sweatshirts, and caps to help fund it. But she isn't complaining. "It's great fun because it's two things I love. I'm helping the Greyhounds and I'm flying my airplane."

McCurry may be one of the more prominent examples of the pleasures that come from helping Greyhounds, but she is not alone. Tens of thousands of people around the US have discovered there are few more rewarding experiences than adopting a retired racing Greyhound. He returns an adopter's love and attention in more than equal measure. An ex-racer is easy to spoil, and people will often pamper him to make up for the deficiencies of farm or track life no matter how much others advise against this.

And be advised that ex-racers are a lot like potato chips: it's hard to have just one.

Your New Greyhound

The Greyhound who comes to you from the racetrack is not a puppy but an adult, fully grown, purebred Greyhound, generally between the ages of 2 and 4, but sometimes as young as 18 months or as old as 5 (the mandatory retirement age). A small female might weigh as few as 40 pounds, while some males will weigh 100 pounds and still be at normal weight. The older the dog, the better racer he was, but whether he was fast enough for a full racing career or too unmotivated to graduate from training to the track will not make him more or less desirable as a pet.

Your Greyhound may or may not come with any paperwork showing his history, but racing and lineage records are available and can be traced by way of ear tattoos, which all racing Greyhounds receive when they are three months old. The tattoos provide proof of a dog's identity to racing officials. The right ear has the birth date, with numbers for the month and year and a letter to show his order in the litter; for example, 32K (March 1992, 11th in the litter) or 112A (November 1992, first in the litter). The number in the left ear is the actual litter registration number. The tattoos sometimes fade, so you may have to do some guessing. With that number, you can contact the National Greyhound Association at (785) 263-4660 and find out the racing name, the date of whelping, and the names of the sire and dam. Information on littermates can sometimes be found

The older your Greyhound is when you adopt him, the better racer he was. However, a Greyhound's skill on the track will not make him more or less desirable as a pet.

through www.rosnet2000.net, where details on the dog's racing career are also sometimes available.

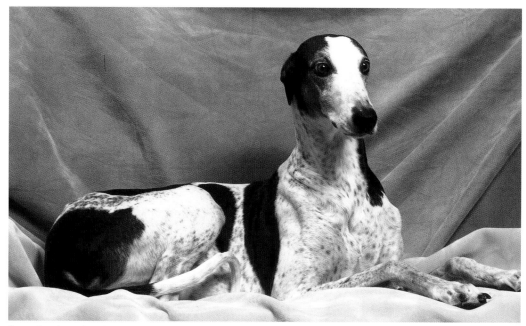

Every Greyhound registered for racing has a card listing identifying characteristics, such as coat color on head, ears, sides, and chest, which make him unique.

Every Greyhound registered for racing has a Bertillon card that lists 56 identifying characteristics, including the ear tattoos, color of each toe nail, and coat color on head, ears, sides, chest, and buttocks that make that racer unique. The color "brindle" refers to the striping pattern visible against another color, such as fawn.

A Racing Greyhound's Life Before Adoption

What was your retired racer's life like before he came to you? He was probably one of five to nine pups in a litter and weighed from three-quarters to one-and-three-quarters pounds. He spent the first year of his life at the breeding farm, where his exercise program started at about two months of age when he was placed in runs of increasing length. When he was a year old, he and his littermates were transferred to a training kennel. Initial training was on a schooling track, where puppies are handheld so that the mechanical lure is always in sight.

During the first couple of schooling sessions, he established a running pattern—inside, outside, fast-breaker, slow-breaker, pacesetter, closer—that he likely used for the rest of his running life. As his ability increased, he graduated to a starting box, longer distances, and increased competition. If he actually made it to a racing kennel—at 17 to 19 months of age—a trainer began working with him so he could qualify for a racing career that may have lasted a few months or a few years.

Adapting To "Pet Life"

If your ex-racer was fostered in someone's home after coming from the track, he was already exposed to the basics of "pet life" and "house manners," taught how to walk up and down a flight of stairs, and learned on his own that some floor surfaces, like wood and vinyl, can be very slippery. He probably also learned a family's routine and adapted to it but should have no trouble adapting to the routine in your household. However, if your ex-racer should come to you directly from a trainer or a track, you will have to undertake the teaching role from the very beginning.

House-manners training requires vigilance and consistent correction while teaching your Greyhound where it is acceptable for him to sleep, how you expect him to behave when guests come, and that he may relieve himself outside only. Crate trained at the track, he knows he is to relieve himself away from his crate; most Greyhounds easily make the connection that a house is basically a giant crate. Ex-racers are easily housetrained from life at the track, where they learned to keep their individual crates clean and to relieve themselves outside on a regular schedule, usually four times a day. Accidents will happen, but far less frequently than with a puppy.

> ## Greyhound Colors
> There are 18 recognized colors in the racing world.
> - Blue brindle
> - Black and white (mostly black)
> - Fawn brindle
> - Brindle
> - Fawn
> - White and black (mostly white)
> - Red brindle
> - Black brindle
> - Red fawn
> - Red and white
> - Light brindle
> - Blue (dark gray)
> - Red
> - White and brindle ticked (predominantly white with brindle patches and spots)
> - Dark brindle
> - Black
> - Dark red
> - White and brindle

Teaching Your Greyhound to Use the Stairs

Greyhounds coming off the track or from a breeding farm have no idea what a set of stairs is or why they have to use it. They have spent their lives on a single level, when the closest they came to ascending stairs was to go into an upper crate (by jumping or being picked up) or into a hauling vehicle. Consequently, your Greyhound may be very scared and uncertain when first introduced to stairs.

To teach your ex-racer how to ascend and descend steps, start with a short flight of stairs, preferably carpeted for better traction. He may try to leap several steps at a time

Because retired racers have spent their lives in a single level environment, people who adopt a Greyhound that came straight from the track will have to teach him to use the stairs.

in either direction, so you will need to keep control of him during this learning process. It helps if there is a wall on one side of the stairs to give him a greater feeling of security and stability. Gravity will assist your Greyhound as he learns to go down steps, but teaching him to go up is best done with two people, one behind and the other in front or at the side, working together to move each of his four feet from step to step, repeating the routine until finally he can do it on his own.

Another method is to stand very close to your Greyhound, grip his collar with your hand held against your leg and begin to walk slowly up the steps so that he has to go along. He will also be able to follow your example as you ascend or descend the stairs, and your presence may make him feel more secure. It may seem at times, as he cowers at the top of the stairs or struggles against your help going up, that he will never get the hang of it. But eventually he will, if for no other reason than that he will soon realize you and he are on different levels of the house, and he wants to get to where you are.

Crate Training

A crate or portable kennel can be an enormously helpful training aid, while also providing the ex-racer a place to call his own. Using a crate at home is not cruel. Your Greyhound was in the crate most hours of every day at the track and has been through many changes since leaving that environment. The familiarity of a crate for the first few days or weeks will help your Greyhound make the transition to pet life.

Some Greyhounds are fearful and hesitant in their new environments and will seek out the crate if the door is left open for them to come and go at will. Their forays into areas where their people are will become more frequent and last longer as they become comfortable in their new surroundings, but much of the time they may still want to curl up inside the familiar crate.

Until you can be sure that your new family member can be trusted and is comfortable out of your sight, a crate can be your best friend. By putting your Greyhound in his crate whenever you have to leave the house, you can rest assured knowing exactly where he is and that he is safe. He may whine, he may even howl, but he will eventually stop. Whatever you do, don't let him out until he is quiet, or you will have taught him that making

Greyhounds tend to develop a close bond with their adopters and may experience separation anxiety when left alone.

noise means getting out. Feeding him in the crate and giving him special toys and treats while inside it can help to make crating a positive experience.

At some point, your new retired racer can be trusted to be on his own at home, without a crate, although some people do crate their Greyhounds whenever they are out of the house. He may experience separation anxiety when left alone— after all, he recently lived in a building with a hundred other racing dogs—and you will have to condition him to

Okay to Crate

The familiarity of a crate for the first few days or weeks will help your Greyhound make the transition to pet life.

understand that you will always return. Again, a crate can be helpful because it can control destructive behavior caused by his anxiety. Using the crate at times other than when you are leaving the house can keep him from only associating crating with your absence. A radio, which some tracks use in their kennels, or a television can be good substitute company and a diversion.

When he first comes to his new home, keep a close eye on him, even attaching the lead to his collar and securing the other end around your waist—that way your hands are free, but you always know where he is. If he does something he shouldn't, you can issue a firm "No!" at the appropriate time. If what he does is urinate in the house, either because he needs to or because he wants to mark, you can say, "No!" then hustle him outside to relieve himself.

Your Greyhound and Your Home

His first experiments in freedom may have some unexpected, even unpleasant, results. The tales of the early days of a new Greyhound often involve finding a mess somewhere in the house. Greyhounds especially enjoy tearing up paper, including

books and magazines—remember, shredded newspaper may have been their only toy at the track. My favorite photograph of an ex-racer's handiwork features a green dog bed on which there are a single blue sock, a hardback book, and many tiny scraps of paper from its cover, which has been artfully torn so that all that can be read of its front is the book title, *When Good Dogs Do Bad Things*.

Your Greyhound may be an adult chronologically, but he didn't really have a puppyhood like other breeds of dogs. Until he passes through that stage, he may chew on wood, whether it's the leg of your

A retired racing Greyhound is often very curious and will want to thoroughly explore his new environment when you first bring him home.

antique table or a stairway newel post, and tear up plastic and paper bags. Like a puppy, he will try getting into anything that looks or smells interesting but, unlike a puppy, his eye/nose level is at the height of the kitchen table.

If you encounter behavior problems you don't know how to solve, rather than despair, remember that when you adopted an ex-racer, you became a member of a human pack that offers a world of support. From the family that fostered your Greyhound, to members of your local adoption group, to e-mails on the Greyhound-List, you will be able to find help—just ask for it. Many others who have adopted ex-racing Greyhounds have probably had the same problems you are experiencing.

Environment and Socialization

The ex-racer is not the dog for everyone. As sight hounds—canines that rely on their keen eyesight to identify prey—Greyhounds have an instinct to chase something moving and therefore cannot be let off lead except in an enclosed area. Also, because of their explosive speed, they should never be tied out in a yard, where they could break their necks if they tried to chase something. As dogs with short hair and almost no body fat, they have little protection against temperature extremes and thus must live inside the house. They often do not bark, so they may be unsuitable as watchdogs. And some people may find the Greyhound's laid-back demeanor too "undoglike." However, in the right environment with proper socialization, retired racing Greyhounds are model pets.

Environment

Some people who have considered adopting an ex-racer say they abandoned the idea because they live in an apartment or don't have a fenced yard large enough for running. While some adoption groups do require that the adopter have a fenced yard, others have found that apartment life and the lack of a fenced yard does not necessarily mean he or she cannot provide a Greyhound with a good home. Greyhounds are large dogs, but they can take up a surprisingly small amount of space. Curled up, some of them could even pass for

With the right environment and proper socialization, a retired racing Greyhound is the ideal pet.

a much smaller breed, although when they stretch out, they can take up a great deal of couch or bed space.

Greyhounds love to nest and will often curl up into a doughnut shape on the nearest couch, carpet, or cushy blanket.

As much as ex-racers might like to run and play outside, Greyhounds are not dogs that can live outdoors. Because of their thin coats, short hair, and low body fat, they have little protection against the elements, hot or cold. Insulated coats, specially designed with a large chest area and length appropriate to the Greyhound physique, can keep them warm in winter. But while these are eye-catching and attractive, they are not necessary. As long as the Greyhound is moving, he will stay warm. But, if the temperature outside is uncomfortable for you, then your Greyhound probably would prefer to be indoors, too.

The fact that they have little insulation and thus little natural padding means Greyhounds prefer to lie down on a soft surface. If it's a hot day, they may stretch out on the wood or vinyl floor because it is cooler, just like any other breed, but mostly they will search out a sofa, carpet, or cushy bed. They enjoy propping their heads on the arm of a couch to watch what is going on from the advantage of height, and they absolutely love to nest. Give yours a blanket, and he will paw and fluff until that blanket has many layers. Then, after circling several times, he will sink with great satisfaction right into the middle of it and curl up in a doughnut shape.

Socialization

Although Greyhounds have regular interaction with people in the racing kennels and on the track, the important thing to remember is that they are not pets when they are at the track. They live in wire crates inside a large kennel building, not in a home with couches, beds, and the social benefits of pet life.

Undoubtedly, there are track and training personnel who physically mistreat Greyhounds, but there are also owners and trainers who are incredibly affectionate with their dogs. Mostly what these wonderful canines endure is neglect—a lack of regular physical and emotional affection and, at the lower-grade tracks where there is little money, a lack of basic grooming and maintenance (hence the extremely long toenails and the ticks and fleas they often have when they come from the track). What is perhaps the single-most surprising fact about retired racing Greyhounds is that, except for the very shy ones, these dogs come off the track and into a house and almost instantly bond with people.

Considering that they are fully-grown adult dogs with no pet-life experience when they come from the track, they adapt incredibly well and easily to their new routine and their new pack—of humans. Their basic easygoing demeanor and sweet nature, which makes Greyhounds easy to handle in large numbers at the track, must be what lets them take so readily to couch-potato life in someone's home. Ex-racers enjoy human affection, attention, and touching, and many of them will actively seek it out, sometimes making it hard for their adopters to get things done. It's not easy to lounge on the bed reading a novel when your Greyhound is lying by your side constantly nudging the hand holding the book so you have to pay attention to him!

An ex-racer's socialization with small animals and children may take a bit longer to develop. After all, they chased a "rabbit" in the race and saw few, if any, children at the track. With time, patience, and a firm "No!" when unwanted behavior is displayed, most retired racers can learn to live and interact appropriately with non-Greyhound pets. The key to their appropriate interactions with children is to make sure the children know how to behave with the Greyhounds.

Each retired racer has his or her individual personality—plus a history from puppyhood to the day he leaves the track that can never be fully known. There is no question that some Greyhounds come off the track fearful. They may run away from people and try to avoid being touched. Gentle handling and a soothing voice can help them to become less frightened, but this socialization process may take many months. Some things can't be rushed. Patience is a must.

Muzzles

Some people think any dog wearing a muzzle is vicious, but for a Greyhound, wearing a muzzle is more like putting on protective athletic gear. When he is muzzled, a Greyhound who is racing around cannot accidentally snag another Greyhound's skin with a tooth and cause a tear. Greyhounds don't have much fur to protect their skin from contact with sharp objects, such as teeth. In the excitement of running and playing, even a normally placid Greyhound may nip at another hound, especially if bumped. Greyhounds are used to wearing muzzles at the track, where they wear ones made of wire, leather, or plastic during a race. Some adoption groups send a Greyhound to his new home with a plastic muzzle and advise adopters to use it when the dog is in an unfamiliar situation, such as being introduced to a child or a small animal. With a muzzle on, a Greyhound can still open his mouth wide and drink water, but he can't accidentally harm a person or another animal. The best advice is: Don't take chances.

Exercise

Greyhounds don't have to run, but many like to, even after retirement. They don't require any more exercise than, for example, a Labrador or a Golden Retriever, and may even need less. A retired racer can be quite happy with a 20-minute walk each day, a longer walk once or twice a week, or regular jogging with a family member. Greyhounds are sprinters, so they should be gradually introduced to distance running to develop endurance. More than one Greyhound adopter has discovered with dismay that the ex-racer is turning the back lawn into an oval dirt track from repeated laps around the yard. If you feel a fondness for grassy expanses, consider fencing off an area for a Greyhound run. It won't have grass for long—their turns send clumps of grass flying through the air—but the grass can be replaced with small, smooth stones or with wood chips to keep down the mud.

And even if he has his own run, your Greyhound will still cherish those walks with you, not for the exercise so much as for the sensory stimulation. Walking around the neighborhood is the Greyhound's equivalent of your reading the front page of the newspaper or watching the evening news—it catches him up on what has been happening in his world while he was out of touch.

Ex-racing Greyhounds are used to a regimen and a structure at the racetrack, where they raced about every third day but spent the vast majority of their time in a crate. They will quickly adapt to lounging around on the furniture at your house, but some form of exercise will keep them fit and help them avoid boredom, which can lead to mischief.

Even though many retired racers still like to run, a 20-minute walk each day with a family member provides a sufficient amount of exercise.

Activities for You and Your Greyhound

Agility

One small but growing activity among Greyhound adopters is agility. The canine equivalent of an obstacle course, agility is a circuit of structures, such as low hurdles, tunnels, a bridge that sways, an elevated bridge (a dogwalk), a teeter-totter to walk across, a series of poles around which the dog must travel in a weaving pattern, and a suspended tire to jump through. It is up to the handler to direct the dog through the course in the correct order, with competitions scored on time and accuracy in completing the prescribed circuit.

An activity that is growing in popularity for Greyhounds is agility, where a dog must successfully find his way through obstacles such as tunnels, low hurdles, and teeter-totters.

Dr. Sharon H. Smith, a founder of Greyhound Rescue Adoption Team (GReAT) in Buffalo, New York, was one of the early adopters to participate in the sport, and her retired racer Duncan was often the only Greyhound at agility meets. Even in 2003, there were probably fewer than 50 retired racing Greyhounds formally competing in agility trials around the United States.

Smith concludes, "Training sighthounds is more difficult than some other breeds. Greyhounds' temperament is less suited to structured training of any sort, not just agility. They're smart, but they're independent. Most of them would just prefer to hang out. It's unusual to find one that wants to run and jump. For most dogs, agility is the ultimate release. Agility is fun, they get to run and they get to play. For Greyhounds, it's (still) a controlled exercise. Its fun, but it's not the ultimate fun for them."

Smith points out that one of the major rewards of agility training is the bonding experience between the adopter and the Greyhound. But it is an off-lead sport and she recommends training and competing in an indoor facility or an outdoor one surrounded by a fence. "Also, make the training sessions short and very positive," she adds. "Find a super treat—food or toy, depending on the dog's motivation—that the dog gets only for training."

Lure Coursing

Perhaps more fun for a Greyhound would be lure coursing. It is conducted in an open field, off-lead, and without a collar or tags, so you must be confident that if your dog loses sight of the lure, he will come to you. This is not to negate the admonition that a Greyhound must be in an enclosed area or on a lead at all times, but lure coursing is an activity that takes place in a controlled situation, and the dog is not actually "running loose." More than 30 states have lure coursing groups. Some are organized by specific breeds (e.g. Whippets, Afghan Hounds or Salukis), while others are organized by the general designation of sight hound (which, of course, includes Greyhounds), or just as lure coursing.

In a departure from the Greyhound's history as a courser, lure coursing today uses no live animals. The lure is generally a white plastic bag or flag attached to a line that is a few inches above the ground. The line is arranged in a continuous loop, powered by a motor; the speed is controlled so that the lure stays just ahead of the

> ## Traveling With Your Greyhound
>
> While it is doesn't necessarily provide much exercise, traveling and vacationing with your Greyhound is a favorite activity of many adopters—and probably their Greyhounds, as well—and it has become much easier as hotels, motels, and even bed-and-breakfast establishments permit guests to bring their pets. There are several books and websites that list pet-friendly accommodations, but the best advice is to check that status before arriving—just in case there has been a change.

Your Greyhound may enjoy running, even though he is retired from racing. If you let your Greyhound run, make sure he does so in an enclosed area.

dogs, which generally race two or three at a time. The lure line operator must be totally focused on the dogs so that he can stop the line if the dogs lose sight of the lure or become entangled in the line, which can cause serious injury. At the finish line, the dogs often reward themselves by pouncing on the bag and ripping it apart in a gleeful frenzy. Spectators can be grateful that the prey is only plastic.

Because lure coursing is physically very demanding, a Greyhound must be in peak running condition before engaging in this activity. Injuries are not uncommon in this taxing sport, which is run on fields that may have holes or other depressions to trip up the dogs. It is not uncommon to see a dog lose his footing and tumble head over heels before getting up to continue the chase. An ex-racer who has been doing nothing but lounging for several months or years since retirement is not a fit candidate for coursing. Contact coursing groups for information on meets, practice sessions, and training.

Dog Daycare

If your Greyhound is an only dog, he might benefit from a recent innovation: daycare for dogs. Canine daycare establishments have sprung up in many cities and provide company for a dog that would otherwise be left home alone while the people are at work. Dogs that might be spending time getting into trouble out of boredom or just lying around out of inertia have an opportunity to socialize with people and other dogs. Many dogs taken to daycare come home exhausted at the end of the day, just like the people they live with.

After adopting a Greyhound, you may wonder just how fast yours can run, even if he failed to advance beyond the first few races. He most likely runs fast, but perhaps only if he wants to—after all, he is retired. Given the opportunity, he may run like the athlete he used to be, or not. Greyhound behavior isn't always predictable.

If you have an opportunity to watch your ex-racer run for fun, be sure the area is enclosed so he doesn't get out of sight or lost. Put a muzzle on him before you let him loose as a precaution if other dogs are present.

Feeding and Nutrition

Greyhounds arrive from the track quite thin, at their racing weight, and people unfamiliar with the ex-racing Greyhound may accuse you of starving your dog or tell you he needs to be fattened up. However, fattening up a Greyhound threatens the dog's health. Aside from the usual dangers obesity poses in any dog, in the Greyhound, with the full weight of his body pounding down onto those slender legs when he runs, the risk of serious injury is high. With proper nutrition after adoption, ex-racers soon put on the extra five to seven pounds that bring them to an appropriate weight for a retiree—any more weight than that is a potential health problem. You should always be able to see the last two ribs on your Greyhound's side; if you can't, cut back on the amount of food and increase the amount of exercise.

Diet

At the track, Greyhounds are usually fed a raw, meat-based diet high in protein and low in fat. Once your adopted Greyhound becomes a "pet," his lifestyle will change sufficiently that he will no longer need such a high-protein diet. Instead, he may need food with a higher percentage of fat so he can gain some weight. Greyhounds are dogs with generally high metabolism, and they burn off calories fairly readily, but an inactive one may still develop a weight problem. The important

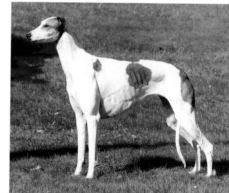

Although Greyhounds may appear thin, this is actually normal for them. You should always be able to see the last two ribs on a Greyhound's side.

thing is to feed your Greyhound a quality dry dog food that doesn't contain a lot of filler. Too much filler will mean a lot of waste outside and does not provide as many of the necessary nutrients.

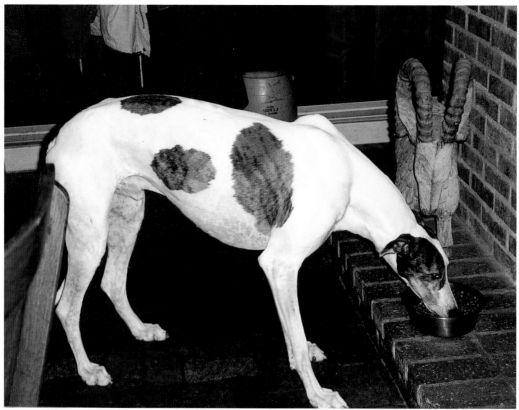

Feed your Greyhound a good-quality, dry dog food that doesn't contain a lot of filler.

Feeding your Greyhound a diet primarily of soft or canned food can lead to dental problems because these foods tend to stick to the teeth. Some dry foods are specifically advertised as a dental aid because they have a larger nugget that requires the dog to chew the hard food, thus scraping the teeth, rather than allowing him to swallow it whole.

Some Greyhounds have delicate digestive systems and may have stools that are very soft, even verging on diarrhea. If that is the case, after your veterinarian confirms that there are no parasitic causes for the soft stool, try a dry food that is made of lamb meal and rice. But anytime you make a change in your dog's diet, introduce the new food gradually. You can do this by mixing the new food with the old and over a period of days or even weeks, reducing the amount of the old food and increasing the amount of the new food.

A high-quality dog food should provide the proper nutrition for your Greyhound, and supplements should not be necessary. If your Greyhound's skin is very dry and flaky or his coat is very coarse, add a tablespoon of corn oil to his food. But be careful it doesn't put on any unwanted weight.

Feeding

Some Greyhounds have such long necks and legs that it is awkward for them to eat from a dish placed on the floor. For them, an elevated dog bowl, available from pet-supply stores or catalogues, may be the answer, or just buy an inexpensive footstool at a discount department store or home store and place the bowl on that. Place a section of slightly tacky shelf covering on the stool to help keep the bowl stationary.

If your Greyhound has a tendency to gulp his food, add some water to slow him down. Many dogs that have just come from the track gobble their food and regurgitate it almost immediately, but moistening the dry food will help prevent that. Sometimes they will snort small dry food nuggets up their noses when they eat too fast. If that happens, switch to a larger nugget. If your Greyhound periodically becomes

> ## Table Manners
>
> Do yourself, your Greyhound, and any dinner guests you have a big favor by not feeding him people food or feeding him from the table. If his treats and meals come from a regular place in the kitchen but not the table, he won't beg at or hang around the table during meals. If you want to give him a periodic people treat, such as cheese or your meat scraps, pretend to get it from the container holding his dog treats.

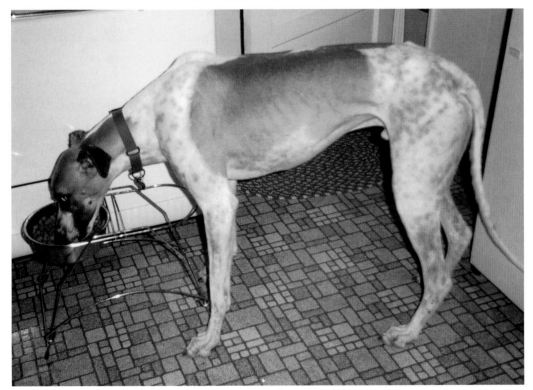

Because the long necks and legs of Greyhounds sometimes make it awkward for them to eat from a dish that is placed on the floor, an elevated dog bowl is probably the best option.

Feed your Greyhound twice a day, in the morning and in the evening, and always wait an hour after exercise before you feed him.

tired of the same old food, spice it up by adding a tablespoon of canned dog food and a little water to make it into gravy.

Greyhounds should be fed twice a day, in the morning and the evening. Their total daily intake is considerable—five or six cups for most males, three or four cups for females and small males—and it is best to split it into two meals. Never feed your Greyhound right after he has exercised and do not let him exercise right after he has eaten—always wait at least an hour. Greyhounds are subject to bloat, a swelling and twisting of the abdomen, which appears to develop because of an accumulation of air and fluid in the stomach that cannot be expelled by burping or vomiting. It occurs after eating and is a "serious, life-threatening problem primarily affecting large-breed, big-chested dogs," according to a medical guide by the University of California at Davis School of Veterinary Medicine. Bloat, also called gastric torsion, should be attended to immediately by a veterinarian. Clinical signs include abdominal distension, retching without vomiting, and excessive salivation.

If you have more than one dog, feed them in different parts of the room and watch them while they eat. Some dogs are protective of their food and will growl and snap. Don't let children bother them during mealtimes.

Always keep plenty of fresh water available and accessible, although leaving a bowl of water in a crate can lead to a watery mess.

A Greyhound's Chewing Needs

Puppies and young Greyhounds need something with resistance to chew on while their teeth and jaws are developing for several reasons. Chewing is necessary for cutting the puppy teeth, inducing growth of the permanent teeth under the puppy teeth, assisting in getting rid of the puppy teeth at the proper time, helping the permanent teeth grow through the gums, ensuring normal jaw development, and settling the permanent teeth solidly in the jaws.

The adult Greyhound's desire to chew stems from the instinct for teeth cleaning, gum massage, and jaw exercise—plus the need for an outlet for periodic doggie tensions. This is why dogs, especially puppies and young dogs, will often destroy property worth hundreds of dollars when their chewing instinct is not diverted from their owner's possessions. And this is why you should provide your Greyhound with something to chew—something that has the necessary functional qualities, is desirable from the Greyhound's viewpoint, and is safe for him.

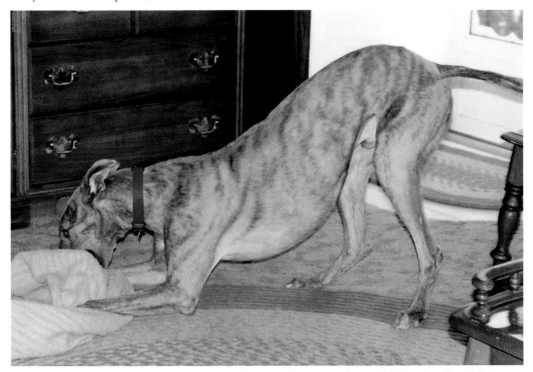

Giving your retired racing Greyhound safe toys or bones to chew on, such as a Nylabone®, will satisfy his chewing instinct and divert his attention away from your possessions.

It is very important that your Greyhound not be permitted to chew on anything he can break or on any indigestible thing from which he can bite sizable chunks. Sharp pieces, such as from a bone, may pierce the intestinal wall and kill the dog. Indigestible things that can be bitten off in chunks, such as from shoes or rubber or plastic toys, may cause an intestinal stoppage (if not regurgitated) and bring painful death unless surgery is promptly performed.

Chew on This

Strong natural bones, such as shin bones from mature beef about 4 to 8 inches in length, may serve your Greyhound's teething needs if his mouth is large enough to handle them effectively. All hard natural bones are very abrasive. If your Greyhound is an avid chewer, natural bones may wear away his teeth prematurely; hence, they should be taken away from your dog when the teething purposes have been served.

Contrary to popular belief, knuckle bones that can be chewed up and swallowed by your Greyhound provide little, if any, usable calcium or other nutriment. They do, however, disturb the digestion of most dogs and cause them to vomit the nourishing food they need.

Greyhounds have an instinct to chew, so make sure you provide your pet with toys that are both fun and safe.

Dried rawhide products of various types, shapes, sizes, and prices are available on the market and have become quite popular. However, they don't serve the primary chewing functions very well; they are a bit messy when wet from mouthing, and most Greyhounds chew them up rapidly—but they have been considered safe for dogs until recently. Now, more and more incidents of death and near-death by strangulation have been reported to be the results of partially swallowed chunks of rawhide swelling in the throat. More recently, some veterinarians have been attributing cases of acute constipation to large pieces of incompletely digested rawhide in the intestine.

A new product, molded rawhide, is very safe. During the process, the rawhide is melted and then injection molded into the familiar dog shape. It is very hard and is eagerly accepted by Greyhounds. The melting process also sterilizes the rawhide. Don't confuse this with pressed rawhide, which is nothing more than small strips of rawhide squeezed together. The nylon bones, especially those with natural meat and bone fractions added, are probably the most complete, safe, and economical answer to the chewing need. Nylabones® are great choices for this type of chew toy. Dogs cannot break them or bite off sizable chunks; hence, they are completely safe—and being longer lasting than other things offered for the purpose, they are economical.

Hard chewing raises little bristle-like projections on the surface of the nylon bones—to provide effective interim tooth cleaning and vigorous gum massage, much in the same way your toothbrush does it for you. The little projections are raked off and swallowed in the form of thin shavings, but the chemistry of the nylon is such that they break down in the stomach fluids and pass through without effect.

The toughness of the nylon provides the strong chewing resistance needed for important jaw exercise and effectively aids teething functions, but there is no teeth wear because nylon is non-abrasive. Being inert, nylon does not support the growth of microorganisms; and it can be washed in soap and water or it can be sterilized by boiling or in an autoclave.

Nylabone® is highly recommended by veterinarians as a safe, healthy, nylon bone that can't splinter or chip. The bone is frizzled by the dog's chewing action, creating a toothbrush-like surface that cleanses the teeth and massages the gums. They are available in your local pet-supply shop and are superior to the cheaper bones because they are made of virgin nylon, which is the strongest and longest-lasting type of nylon available. The cheaper bones are made from recycled or re-ground nylon scraps and have a tendency to break apart and split easily.

Nothing, however, substitutes for periodic professional attention for your Greyhound's teeth and gums. Have your Greyhound's teeth cleaned at least once a year by your veterinarian, and he will be happier, healthier, and far more pleasant to live with. He will have to be given anesthesia for this dental cleaning, and, as always with Greyhounds, the appropriate anesthetic is a must.

Training Your Greyhound

An ill-behaved dog is unwelcome almost anywhere, and this is true even if the dog is as elegant as an ex-racing Greyhound. Any dog can benefit from the instruction of obedience training or the routine of obedience classes. Obedience training is especially important when a dog is as strong, large, and muscular as the Greyhound, weighing as much as 85 to 100 pounds.

Obedience Training

Although training classes usually put metal choke collars on the dogs, this is unnecessary for almost all Greyhounds. Racing Greyhounds are walked on lead at the track prior to a race, and thus many of the ex-racers are, from the start, easy to walk on a lead at your left side. But some were not easy to walk at the track and some just regard every outing as a chance to tug you down the street toward the slightest motion. Both the owner and the Greyhound can benefit greatly from the dog's learning four basic commands: sit, heel, stay, and come. When training your Greyhound to follow these commands, keep in mind that training should be very positive and in short sessions, or your Greyhound will quickly lose motivation and interest.

Even the elegant Greyhound can benefit from obedience training, particularly the four basic commands: sit, heel, stay, and come.

All the commands should be one or two words at most, said in a happy tone of voice. For instance, never say, "Sit, sit, sit" because this only teaches your Greyhound to wait for the command to be repeated before responding.

The Sit Command

For the Greyhound, the hardest command to learn is the sit command. Whether it is because of their conditioning at the track or because of their unique body structure, it

is no easy task to get even the most cooperative Greyhound to sit. If the Greyhound also happens to be stubborn, the job is really tough. In fact, one obedience teacher with many years of Greyhound experience tells Greyhound owners who enroll in her class that if, in the nine weeks of the course, the ex-racer learns nothing more than how to sit on command, the course will have been a success for that dog. Greyhounds sit with their weight fully on the lower part of their hind legs and their rear ends do not rest on the floor, so perhaps they don't find sitting a very comfortable position.

So, what's the secret to teaching a Greyhound to sit? There probably isn't one. You can push down on a Greyhound's rear

Teaching a Greyhound to sit is usually the most difficult obedience command, perhaps due to their unique body structure.

end until your arms ache, and that might do it. Or, easier on you both, you can use a scoop movement, reaching your left arm behind the Greyhound's rear legs where you want them to bend and pulling your arm forward. The area behind the knee joint is a weaker area on which to exert pressure. Another way is to hold a treat right over your Greyhound's nose and move your hand and the treat back in the direction of his tail, so that he has to shift his balance toward his rear end as he raises his nose. No matter which method you use, you can teach him to sit on command by saying, "Sit" whenever he accomplishes the movement of sitting.

The Heel Command

When a dog heels, he walks closely by your side, turning as you turn. If the dog lags or pulls, use food or a toy (whatever motivates your dog) held close to the dog's nose and say, "Heel." As the Greyhound stays at your side, intermittently give him a treat. Reward all positive behavior with your voice and a treat. Ignore all inappropriate

When you teach your Greyhound to heel, he will walk or trot closely by your side, matching his pace with yours.

behavior. It is not necessary to use any collar correction. When heeling, the Greyhound should match his pace to yours as he stays at your side. As he becomes more proficient at this, you can vary from a walk to a fast walk or trot. Remember to consistently reward your Greyhound for following the command.

The Stay Command

Start out by having your Greyhound sit. Put your left hand out flat in front of his face and say, "Stay." Don't use his name as part of the command. Then still holding the lead, walk a few steps forward and turn to face him. Initially, the dog should be told to "stay" for very brief periods—a matter of seconds— and then reward him for the behavior.

Be Positive

Greyhounds are extremely sensitive, and a voice that is too loud or a tone that is too harsh can set back training irreparably. Their feelings can actually be hurt if they are handled indelicately, either by word or deed. Positive reinforcement and praise are absolutely essential in training, and persistence and patience are incredibly important when teaching a Greyhound obedience. However, it is also important to know when your dog's attention span has reached its limit.

If he gets up or moves toward you, gently put him back at the spot you originally left and tell him to "stay" for an even shorter period. If he stays, reward him by voice, saying, "Good dog!" and give him a treat. Slowly lengthen the time you ask him to stay.

The come command should be taught when you have good control over your Greyhound and can reward him immediately for coming to you.

The Come Command

This should be taught when you have good control of your Greyhound and can reward him immediately. Start from the stay command and step away from your Greyhound until you are at the end of a 4- to 6-foot lead and facing him. Say the command, "Come!" in a happy excited voice. Reward him for coming to you. When he comes consistently at your command, use a longer lead so that you are farther apart. Eventually, you can drop the lead altogether and call him from 30 or 40 feet away. But don't do this in an unenclosed area—even if he has obedience titles.

Obedience Classes

If your Greyhound shows an aptitude for education and you are interested in obedience competition, you can put him into advanced obedience classes and eventually he can earn rating as a companion dog and maybe even win awards.

Obedience classes are offered by dog training clubs, which have their own facilities or use other venues such as schools; by individuals; and even by some pet-supply stores. Other Greyhound owners or the group from which you adopted your dog can direct you to trainers who are familiar with Greyhounds and their special training needs. A shy Greyhound can benefit enormously from the social interaction of a formal obedience class. One-on-one training is also available, usually at your home, but it is more expensive than a class with other dogs. Under no circumstances should you turn your dog over to someone else for training out of your presence. Since a major facet of obedience training is teaching the human how to interact with the dog, you should be involved every step of the way.

An added incentive to ensuring that you have a well-behaved Greyhound is the opportunities it will present for you and your ex-racer to serve as ambassadors to the world at large through a myriad of activities available in the adoption community. Many people who see a well-behaved, beautiful Greyhound at your side might be curious enough to ask some questions and end up adopting, too.

The image of retired racers is a strongly positive one, and everyone involved with retired racing Greyhounds as pets wants to keep it that way.

Grooming Your Greyhound

With their extremely short hair and little shedding, Greyhounds are easy to maintain. However, brushing, bathing, nail clipping, dental care, and ear cleaning are aspects of grooming that should be made a part of your Greyhound's regular care program. The following information outlines how to go about taking these necessary grooming steps.

Brushing

Regular brushing is important because it removes what hair is shed and releases oils in the skin to prevent dryness and keep the dog's coat soft. Brushing is also a way for you and your Greyhound to enjoy quality time together since most Greyhounds love to be touched.

A grooming mitt, which can turn brushing time into a massage, a rubber curry brush, or a soft bristle brush are best because they will not scratch the skin. Some Greyhounds have very thin coats, which can easily be brushed with the mitt or curry brush, while others with denser coats may need a bristle brush to remove any loose hair.

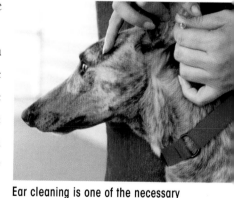

Ear cleaning is one of the necessary aspects of grooming that should be a part of your Greyhound's regular care, along with brushing, bathing, nail clipping, and dental care.

Ear Care

Although ear infections are not especially common in Greyhounds, they do occur. Regular cleaning of the ear with cotton balls, plus the use of an alcohol-free cleaning/drying agent (from your veterinarian), can keep the ears free of wax that can trap germs and lead to infection. If your Greyhound is flapping his head and

Because their extremely short hair does little shedding, Greyhounds are easy to maintain. However, if your Greyhound gets muddy or dirty, you should bathe him using dog-formulated shampoo.

digging at an ear, you'd better take a look. Then clean the outer ear area and the canal as your veterinarian has directed; if the problem persists, you may need to have your veterinarian examine your Greyhound's ears and possibly prescribe an antibiotic ointment or drops.

Bathing

Because Greyhounds are indoor dogs and may very well be sleeping in your bed when you are out and even when you are in it, bathing your dog every few months is a good idea. Fortunately, Greyhounds are generally not plagued by a so-called "doggy odor." If your dog gets muddy, let the mud dry and brush it off. Brindle-colored Greyhounds don't show dirt much, but Greyhounds with white in their coats sometimes look "dingy" and benefit from a brightener shampoo. The shampoo you use should be designed specifically for dogs. Human shampoo is too harsh and may cause skin irritation. If it is flea season, bathe your Greyhound only with a pyrethrin-based shampoo. Be careful not to get water in his ears; pack them with cotton balls and cover the ears with your hand while rinsing his head.

Nail Clipping

If you cut your Greyhound's nails once a week or every two weeks, you can take off less at a time and generally avoid nipping the quick, which causes the nail to bleed and can be painful. Many Greyhounds will simply lie on their sides and let you trim their

nails; for others, you may need to have someone hold the dog and his paw steady while you cut.

There are two types of implements for cutting nails: a nail clipper, which resembles small pruning shears but restricts how far up the nail you can cut; and the nail trimmer, which lets you make either a substantial trim or practically "shave" the nail a little at a time. Regardless which kind you use, you may find it necessary to file the edges of the cut nail since some Greyhounds have large nails that can be very sharp when

Because retired racers spend most of their time lounging, their nails do not wear down naturally. Therefore, you should clip your Greyhound's nails once every week or every two weeks.

cut. An emery board does the job very well. Change the cutting blade on the trimmer often—a dull blade will splinter or squeeze the nail rather than making a clean cut. Your Greyhound's nail color may make the job harder or easier; it is difficult to see where the quick is on a darker nail. If the nail bleeds, pour a bit of styptic powder (available from a pet-supply store) in the palm of your hand and press the bleeding nail into the powder. An alternative to either the nail clipper or trimmer is an electric nail grinder, available by mail order. It minimizes splintering and rough edges, but some dogs are frightened by the noise.

Dental Care

Because ex-racing Greyhounds tend to have worse teeth than most other breeds, the importance of good dental hygiene cannot be overstated. Like people, dogs get gingivitis (inflammation of the gums caused by bacteria) and can lose teeth without proper care. Gingivitis is also a primary cause of bad breath in canines. You may see in your veterinarian's office a large, colorful—and frankly frightening—graphic showing different stages of gum disease in canines. Try to recall it whenever you think brushing your dog's teeth is too much trouble. You don't want to see a toothless dog, especially not your own. Many dogs arrive fresh from the track with extremely repugnant breath and teeth that are brown from plaque. Veterinarians often do a thorough teeth cleaning when they spay or neuter the Greyhound, and once that is done, maintenance is up to you.

Giving your Greyhound dog biscuits or a Nylabone® may help with some of the plaque buildup, but there is no substitute for brushing at least once a week, and preferably more often. Use a soft, bristle toothbrush and a canine tooth paste, usually flavored with chicken or beef. This can be a real treat for your dog, who will find the taste so delicious he will try to chew on the brush. Dental kits are also available, containing toothpaste and a small rubber brush that can be put over your index finger.

Your Greyhound may not like you touching his mouth, but you can gradually accustom him to a toothbrushing procedure. At first, just put some of the tasty, flavored toothpaste on your finger and let him lick it off. Do this a few times so he thinks it is a treat. Then put toothpaste on the finger brush and run that over his teeth, quickly at first and then for longer periods of time on subsequent occasions. Soon you will be brushing all his teeth—on a regular basis.

Some Greyhound owners have found their dogs will tolerate the use of an electric toothbrush, which can be much quicker than using a normal human toothbrush, and will even lie still so that plaque can be scraped from teeth with a dental instrument, called a scaler. After brushing, or scaling, teeth, spray an oral solution containing chlorhexidine into his mouth to cut down on bacteria. Small pads treated with chlorhexidine can be wiped over the dog's teeth to eliminate oral bacteria. Check with your veterinarian or pet-supply outlet for availability of any of these.

Generally, a Greyhound will stand or lie still while you work the brush around in his mouth, peeling his lips back with your fingers, and many Greyhounds are so laid-back, they don't even mind if you use a dental scaler to scrape off plaque that builds up in spite of brushing. Regular brushing and scaling will save you money and potential heartache. When a dog's teeth are cleaned at the veterinary clinic, the dog is anesthetized, a procedure that is never without some risk.

You can also combat breath odor with a spray that kills bacteria in the dog's mouth. This is available from a veterinarian or from mail-order pet-supply companies.

Your Greyhound's Health

hen you adopt an ex-racer, you can be comfortable knowing you have seen to his welfare by providing him with a loving home. However, in addition to his welfare, you are responsible for his health. The most important step in maintaining your Greyhound's health is to know your pet. Establish his level of good health and take him to his veterinarian when there is a significant deviation from that norm.

Pay close attention to your Greyhound's normal energy level and functions, so you will recognize if he is abnormally lethargic, panting excessively, losing weight, or experiencing other symptoms that could signal a more serious problem. As you become more experienced as a Greyhound owner, you can separate the serious symptoms from the trivial, but if you are ever in doubt, always consult your veterinarian to determine if what you have noticed is significant.

Pay close attention to your Greyhound's normal energy level and functions; that way you can recognize if there are any changes that could signify a more serious problem.

Finding a Veterinarian

Many adoption/rescue groups have specific veterinarians who work with them to spay/neuter dogs arriving from the track and to give them a medical workup, including vaccinations, testing for internal parasites and tick-borne diseases, teeth cleaning and, if necessary, removal of rotten teeth. The adoption group will provide you with the documentation for all of these procedures. If you decide to entrust your Greyhound's medical care to a different veterinarian than the one who saw him initially, you should make an appointment within

Because of a Greyhound's thin, athletic build, anesthesia can be risky and should be discussed with your veterinarian before it is administered.

a few weeks after adoption to establish your Greyhound's baseline health and to create a relationship between the doctor and your dog.

Thereafter, you should take your Greyhound to his vet annually, and, as he ages, semi-annually. His vaccinations—rabies, canine distemper/parvovirus, CAV-2 hepatitis, and parainfluenza—must be kept up to date. Because an ex-racer's medical history is frequently unavailable when he retires, the rabies vaccination given after he comes from the track should be repeated one year later, as if he has never been vaccinated against rabies. After that, it can be given on the normal three-year cycle.

Anesthesia

One of the things you will want to discuss with your veterinarian is the use of anesthesia on your Greyhound. The literature about retired racing Greyhounds has long cited risks associated with anesthesia use. This is less of a problem now than it was a few years ago, primarily because very few veterinarians still use barbiturates as a preliminary anesthetic so a dog can be intubated for surgery. Since barbiturates are absorbed into fatty tissue, of which

Greyhounds have little, the drugs would enter the Greyhound's bloodstream and render him unconscious for several days. Dr. Harry Newman, a veterinarian who cares for a large Greyhound population in his veterinary practice in Amherst, New York, says the earlier recommendation was that only Isoflurane be used on

Veterinary Care

If you decide to entrust your Greyhound's medical care to a different veterinarian than the one who saw him initially, you should make an appointment within a few weeks after adoption to establish your Greyhound's baseline health and to create a relationship between the doctor and your dog.

Greyhounds, but now the protocol is to use intravenous valium and ketamine in combination, or Propafal, as a pre-anesthetic, then Isoflurane or the newer Sevoflurane. It is probably the rare veterinarian who has not seen a Greyhound in his practice, but just to be safe, you should inquire as to what anesthesia is used by your Greyhound's doctor.

Common Medical Problems

There are a number of common medical problems that can affect retired racers. Greyhound owners should be aware of these problems, so treatment can be sought as soon as possible. Remember, always consult your veterinarian if you think your Greyhound is suffering from any of these health problems.

Abnormal Hair Loss

A great many retired racing Greyhounds come off the track with hair absent from the backs of their thighs. Hair may also be missing from the bottom of the chest. The exact cause of this is not really known, but Newman cites trauma to the thighs and bottom of the chest as a possibility. According to Newman, spending more than 20 hours a day cramped in cages, sitting on their thighs and resting on their chests may "mechanically cause the hair follicle to give up and release the hair."

The constant stress of their racing workouts may also be a cause, says Newman. This stress can cause the adrenal glands to put out a lot of cortisone (a condition called Cushing's disease), so they may be getting stress-related Cushing's disease that could cause premature hair loss.

Thyroid Problems

The thyroid, located in the front of the windpipe, produces hormones that regulate the body's metabolism. Most abnormalities are due to under- or overproduction of these hormones. Hormone levels can be checked through a blood test.

Greyhounds tend to have slow-acting thyroids, a condition that can also result in hair loss. Newman says that it was once thought that all Greyhounds have slow-acting thyroids, "when in fact they just don't have levels of thyroids that equal other dogs." He doubts the percentage of Greyhounds with slow-acting thyroids is higher than in any other breed population. "They just run lower levels of thyroid hormone normally."

So how does a veterinarian decide which Greyhound actually does have a thyroid deficiency? Newman says: "I go by not just what the lab says, but what the dog says." If the dog is lethargic, is intolerant to the cold and is always seeking warmth, has hair loss in different areas, and his thyroid levels don't even register, thyroid supplements are probably called for, he says. But he notes that since retired racers have bald spots anyway and are often quiet, it is not always clear that this is indicative of thyroid disease. In those gray areas, he says, thyroid supplements can be given for two months to see if there is a significant difference. "If there is, then they are hypothyroid. If there's no difference at all, then they're not and you can safely stop" the supplement.

Diarrhea

Diarrhea is one of the most common complaints when Greyhounds first come off the track. Having subsisted on a diet of low-quality, ground, raw meat, Greyhounds will frequently experience digestive difficulties when their diet is changed to a more balanced, high-quality dry food. If the diarrhea persists or becomes uncontrolled, the veterinarian should be advised so treatment can be started with an antibiotic. If it appears simply to be because the Greyhound ate something he should not have, an over-the-counter medication can be given, but the dosage should be checked with the veterinarian to avoid overdosing.

Neck Pain

Dr. Newman says this probably is from a pinched nerve and probably related to racing. Racers collide on the track and take a tumble, and the neck pain may be related to an injury that occurred then. The problem comes and goes, he says, but responds to cortisone and pain-relieving drugs. Consult your veterinarian if you think your Greyhound suffers from neck pain.

Urinary Incontinence

This often occurs in mature females and may be just part of the aging process, or it may be a result of the hormones they were given during their racing careers to prevent their going into heat. It can be treated with hormone-replacement therapy.

One recommended solution to separation anxiety is to adopt a second retired racing Greyhound to keep the first one company.

Separation Anxiety

Dr. Newman calls this the biggest problem of dogs going into new homes. Greyhounds have never been alone at the track, he explains, and suddenly they may be the only dog in a household and find themselves left home alone by their humans. The result can be destructive behavior if the dog is free to roam the house or injury to the dog if he is crated and tries desperately to get out.

Although this is a behavioral problem that with time, patience, and sometimes professional help can be corrected, it can also require medical intervention if the condition is too severe. Treatment is with an anti-anxiety drug on a temporary basis. Dr. Newman, who is a Greyhound adopter himself, says his recommendation is to adopt a second Greyhound to keep the first one company.

Epileptic Seizures

A seizure is caused by uncontrolled electrical discharges in the brain, which then stimulates abnormal movement. If the electrical activity is confined to just one area of the brain, a partial seizure results, and the abnormal movements may only be facial twitching, blinking, or jerking of one limb. If the entire brain is affected (called a generalized seizure) the dog will lose consciousness and develop muscle rigidity followed by whole body muscle jerking, sometimes salivation, and often incontinence of urine and stool. Your vet will give you guidelines and possibly medication depending upon the type and cause of the seizure. Seizures are frightening but usually stop on their own within a few minutes. A seizure that does not stop requires emergency treatment. Seizures may be genetic and can be treated with anti-seizure medications.

Corns on the Pads of the Foot

Dr. Newman says he sees this in Greyhounds more than in other breeds. The corn is a projection of hard tissue on the pad that is pushed into it every time the dog steps on that foot. "It's like slowly driving a nail into the pad," he says, "so it gets quite painful." A dog with this problem will limp and favor that foot, but sometimes it is difficult to tell what the problem is until you feel the pad, which is soft except for one spot that is hard, Dr. Newman says. The corn usually must be removed surgically. If you discover a corn on one of your Greyhound's food pads, consult your veterinarian.

To keep your Greyhound's skin and coat healthy, brush his coat regularly and add a tablespoon of corn oil to his food to improve his skin condition.

Dermatitis

Greyhounds have delicate skin, and many ex-racers come from the track with flea allergy dermatitis (skin inflammation), scabs from flea bites, flaky skin, and places on their backs where the hair is sparse and dry. Once the flea problem has been brought under control, the scabs should disappear and the coat should fill in. The Greyhound's flaky skin condition can be improved by adding a tablespoon of corn oil, which has essential fatty acids, to his food, although many quality dog foods now contain Omega 3 fatty acids. Regular brushing of your dog's coat will also help.

Urinary Infections

Urinary infections are not uncommon in dogs because of licking that can spread bacteria from the anus to the urethra. If your Greyhound inexplicably has a change in urination habits or an accident in the house, an infection could be the cause. Take a urine sample to your veterinarian for analysis and possible treatment with an antibiotic.

Lupoid Onchodystrophy

This is an abnormality in the nail bed. The dog will have raw and bleeding toenails and may also lose nails. Newman says he has seen this in a dozen retired racers and only in one dog of another breed. It cannot be cured but can be controlled with treatment: fatty acids Omega 3, Omega 6, niacinamide, tetracycline, and corticosteroids. Consult your veterinarian if you suspect this problem so he or she can prescribe a treatment.

Blood values

Greyhounds show different blood values than other breeds. They have a much higher red blood cell count (this allows them to take in more oxygen and gives them their athletic ability); a lower number of platelets that help blood to clot; and a lower number of white blood cells that fight infection. Newman, who has done preliminary veterinary workups on more than a thousand Greyhounds fresh off the track, says it is important that veterinarians are aware of these different values so a Greyhound is not erroneously perceived as diseased on the basis of these readings.

Parasites

Coming off the track, Greyhounds often have a variety of external and internal parasites that must be eradicated. The dog might be loaded with ticks, which are usually removed after he comes into the hands of an adoption group, and he might have internal parasites as well, such as whipworms, roundworms, tapeworms, and/or hookworms.

Heartworms

Dogs contract heartworm disease from the bite of the mosquito, and the only way to confirm if a dog is infected is through a blood test. If the test is negative, your Greyhound should be given a preventative that is administered monthly until the mosquito season is over (your vet can advise you on how late into the year your Greyhound should receive the medication in your geographic area). Some veterinarians say giving the heartworm test every other year is sufficient, so long as the preventative treatment has been used on a regular schedule and the dog has not been in an area where there is a high incidence of heartworm disease.

In no case should a Greyhound just off the track be given a heartworm preventative without first having a blood test to determine he does not have the disease. There are brands of heartworm preventatives that have the added benefit of controlling other parasites as well, such as roundworm, hookworm, and whipworm.

Ticks

Depending on the geographic location from which your retired racer came, he may have been exposed to a tick-borne disease such as Rocky Mountain spotted fever, Lyme disease, ehrlichiosis or babesiosis. These rickettsial (a type of bacteria) infections can linger with few symptoms, only to cause health problems later. Adoption groups in several parts of the

Tick Exposure in Retired Racers

Greyhounds have no predisposition to tick-borne diseases, but there does seem to be a strong indication of past exposure in ex-racers. Racing Greyhounds are not treated for ticks at the track, judging by the numbers of ticks that are found on dogs coming from the racetracks in many parts of the country. Anywhere there are ticks, these diseases can be found.

Any time your Greyhound goes outside, especially near high grass or trees, carefully check him for ticks or other parasites.

country have newly arrived retired racers tested for titers, which is a measure of antibodies that tells if the dog has in the past been exposed to one of the tick-borne diseases. The results of these tests do not, however, tell whether the disease is there. Newman says most low titers indicate past disease but not current disease, while an extremely high titer can mean the dog has just recovered from the disease or is currently infected. Treatment depends on the type of tick disease indicated by the titers and includes the antibiotic tetracycline.

If you find ticks on your Greyhound, remove them with tweezers and put them into a jar containing alcohol. Ticks are robust and even stepping on them may leave them viable. Be careful to get the head, which is attached to the dog's skin, as well as the body of the tick, and don't handle the tick with your hands or you risk infection yourself.

Fleas

Remove fleas with a flea comb and dip the comb containing the captured fleas in alcohol or flea shampoo. If you bathe your Greyhound with a tick or flea shampoo, be certain it is pyrethrin based. In the case of fleas, a bath only takes care of the adult fleas on your dog at that time. If you want more extensive protection, as well as control over pre-adult fleas, you have to treat your Greyhound and your premises, especially carpets and bedding.

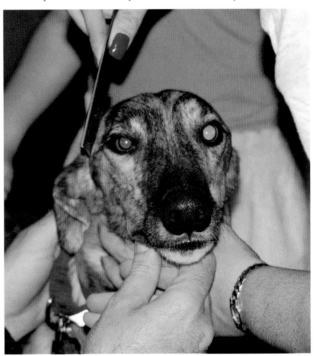

To remove fleas, use a flea comb on your Greyhound's fur. Then dip the comb with the captured fleas into alcohol or flea shampoo.

Many breeds of dog wear flea/tick collars and take oral flea preventatives without adverse health consequences, but for Greyhounds, there seems to be a lack of consensus about the safety of using these methods. While some adoption groups strongly discourage the use of a flea/tick collar or an oral preventative, other medical experts familiar with the Greyhound think this may be unjustified. In any case, collars and oral treatment, which some veterinarians prescribe but others do not, are really unnecessary. Topical treatments dispensed by veterinarians are readily available and considered safe for use with Greyhounds, and flea-control products are continually being developed and introduced for use in dogs. For your Greyhound's protection, if a product for tick or flea control cites a long-lasting effect, or if you have any doubts at all about its safety, check with a Greyhound-knowledgeable veterinarian before using it.

Stool Parasites

Because some parasites are spread by stool, you should pick up after your Greyhound as soon as he relieves himself in your yard as well as in any other private or public area where you walk your dog. An added bonus of making this a habit at home is that you will never have to worry about your Greyhound eating his stool, a habit called coprophagy. Behaviorists have many theories on why dogs do this and there are several possible solutions, including preparations that can be added to a dog's food. But the only sure solution seems to be picking up the feces immediately. If it isn't there, it can't be consumed.

Wounds and Injuries

Greyhounds can come from the track looking pretty banged up, with healing lacerations, lack of hair on their thighs, very visible scars on their torsos (from unsutured tears in the skin), a tail that is crooked or shortened by amputation because it was broken, or even a missing toe because an injury required amputation. However, none of these physical blemishes should be seen to detract from a Greyhound's suitability as a pet and loving companion.

Greyhounds easily suffer L-shaped skin tears on their torsos because their skin is tautly stretched over their muscles and skeletons and there isn't a lot of give. Those scars that many Greyhounds have when they come from the track are from such wounds that were not sutured. If you want to avoid such scarring, have your veterinarian suture a new tear.

If your Greyhound has a tendency to lick a sore or chew off bandages, put his muzzle on; it will help discourage his licking of the injured area. If a laceration is on his upper torso, you can put a T-shirt on him with his front legs through the arm holes and knot the shirt above his back to secure it. If the laceration is at the rear of his body, put his tail through the neck hole and his rear legs through the arm holes and secure the shirt by tying a piece of narrow rope around his waist. You'll have to remove this when your Greyhound goes outside to relieve himself.

Dental Problems

In a word, the teeth of retired racers are terrible. Between their diet of raw meat—known as 4-D meat (from dead, dying, decayed, or diseased animals)—and their lack of any dental care, it is no wonder that so many of them have heavy tartar buildup, extremely foul breath, and need to have teeth removed at their first dental cleaning and often on subsequent occasions as they age. Once a first professional cleaning is done—under anesthesia—the best thing you can do for your Greyhound is brush his teeth regularly. Every day is best, but even three times a week is better than not brushing, medical experts say.

The importance of dental care cannot be overemphasized. Not only does the buildup of tartar lead to gum disease (gingivitis) and subsequent tooth loss, but left unchecked, periodontal disease can allow bacteria to enter the dog's bloodstream. Dogs can develop liver, kidney, and heart disease that must then be treated, but which can also be fatal.

It is important to maintain your retired racing Greyhound's oral health and to brush his teeth regularly.

Diseases

All dogs can contract diseases, and Greyhounds are certainly no exception. No list of medical problems that can occur in ex-racers can be exhaustive, but if you think your Greyhound is suffering from any of the following diseases, consult your veterinarian immediately.

Cancer

Perhaps the worst news that any Greyhound adopter can hear is that his dog has some form of cancer. This sounds like a death sentence, and unfortunately, it often is. Although other forms of cancer, like lymphoma, will occur in Greyhounds, osteosarcoma, or bone cancer, seems to be the predominant type. Usually it is discovered because the dog has a painful limp. Unfortunately, because the limping may be intermittent and thus thought to be just a mild sprain, it may be that by the time the limping is truly persistent and a diagnosis of cancer is made, the cancer may have spread into the chest and the organs.

Treatment can be radiation, amputation, chemotherapy, or simply medication to make the dog comfortable until the situation becomes too serious to let the dog linger. Deciding to pursue one or more of these courses is the most difficult decision a Greyhound adopter may ever face. What the proper course is for one person or Greyhound is not for another. Many Greyhounds who have undergone amputation go on to live for months, even years, and maintain a good quality of life, while others may die within weeks. You and your veterinarian must weigh the options in deciding how to proceed. One of your responsibilities as an adopter is to give your Greyhound a humane death when the quality of life has deteriorated too much.

The causes of canine cancer and the optimal treatments for the various forms are not truly known. Since 1998, The Greyhound Project has had a matching fund program

---

Cancer Symptoms

The Veterinary Cancer Society lists the following symptoms as the ten most common signs of cancer in animals:

- Abnormal swellings that persist or continue to grow
- Sores that do not heal
- Weight loss
- Loss of appetite
- Bleeding or discharge from any body opening
- Offensive odor
- Difficulty eating or swallowing
- Hesitation to exercise or loss of stamina
- Persistent lameness or stiffness
- Difficulty breathing, urinating or defecating

Any of these signs may be an indication of some entirely different problem, but if you see them in your Greyhound, take him in for a check-up and talk to your veterinarian.

Keep your Greyhound on a lead or in an enclosed area anytime he is outdoors.

with the Morris Animal Foundation to support the Greyhound Cancer Project. Into mid-2003, this effort had raised $100,000. The Greyhound Project is supporting studies such as using Endostatin to reduce tumor growth in soft tissue cancer and using a combination of chemotherapy and limb-sparing in bone cancer.

"Several of us lost dogs (to cancer)," says Joan Belle Isle, president of The Greyhound Project. "It was a way to give and help and do something constructive instead of just feeling bad about it." Based on what is currently known, she says, "Greyhounds are no more susceptible (to osteosarcoma) than any other large dog, and in some cases less so," but "we tend to talk about it more" in the Greyhound community.

Inflammatory Bowel Disease (IBD)

Symptoms are primarily recurring diarrhea with occasional vomiting. Consult your veterinarian immediately if you notice these symptoms. Treatment is a low-grade antibiotic, or if that is not effective, your vet may prescribe a stronger antibiotic in the same class of erythromycin; it is used in small animals for its anti-inflammatory properties in the large intestine rather than for its ability to fight infection. Make sure your veterinarian monitors your dog's condition.

Your Greyhound's Safety

There are many ways your Greyhound's safety can be imperiled, outdoors and even inside the house. Remember that, in many cases, a house is a totally new experience for him, but even if he has some house-savvy, he will still be curious about his new environment.

Outdoors Safety

Any time a Greyhound is outdoors, he must be in an enclosed area or on a lead. Otherwise, if he sees something and gives chase, you, a mere human, will never catch up. And because he is so fast and uses sight rather than smell to follow, he may within minutes be so far away that he will be unable to find his way home.

In addition, ex-racers, with their early limited exposure to the world, are ignorant of traffic and can dash into a street filled with vehicles in an instant. No dog should be tied outside, especially not a Greyhound. Because of the explosive force with which they launch a run, being attached to a fixed object can break their necks, so keep your Greyhound fenced in. An invisible fence that uses a shock or loud noise to deter an

In order to keep your retired racer safe from home hazards, monitor anything he chews on and keep anything easily swallowed or toxic out of reach.

animal from leaving an area is not recommended; a Greyhound can run so fast he will be long gone before he even notices the sensation. And an invisible fence does nothing to keep other animals from coming onto your property and attacking your Greyhound.

A normal fence with a height of four or five feet is sufficient; Greyhounds are not jumpers and are not inclined to hurdle a fence. And make sure your ex-racer is always wearing identification tags on a collar specifically designed for his unique anatomy.

Home Hazards

As with children, keep small, easily swallowed items and anything that could be toxic out of sight and out of reach. You may have to put the items up higher for a Greyhound, but don't take any chances. They can rip up boxes and chew through plastic containers with incredible ease, and some Greyhounds have even come close to unscrewing a previously unopened jar. Houseplants, such as amaryllis, hyacinth, poinsettias, and dieffenbachia (dumbcane) are also hazardous. Outdoors, daffodils, foxglove, lily of the valley, rhododendron, yew, honeysuckle, holly, and mistletoe all pose a danger to your Greyhound. Never

Salt that is used to melt ice or snow can be harmful to your Greyhound, so rinse his feet in water if he has walked where the snow has been cleared.

give your dog chocolate, and keep acetaminophen and other medications out of reach. Should you fear that your dog has ingested a foreign and dangerous substance, call your local poison control center or veterinarian for advice immediately.

Salt that is used to melt snow and ice can also be harmful to your Greyhound and to any dog. If you walk your dog in areas where snow or ice has been cleared, always rinse his feet off in water when you get home, so he won't ingest salt while licking his paws.

Check your Greyhound's pads, feet, and legs for cuts after he has been running outdoors. This is particularly important if he was running in a large area that you could not examine completely. Sharp stones, sticks, thorns, and pieces of glass can cause cuts that should be thoroughly cleaned with soap and water and possibly treated with an antibiotic ointment, then covered with gauze and secured with "vet wrap," a stretchy bandaging tape available from pet-supply stores.

Safe Collars for Greyhounds

You probably have noticed that the Greyhound's neck is larger than his head, and his ears lay very flat against the sides and back of his head (until something catches his attention and those ears stand up and swivel like tiny radar dishes). A fixed-length collar that would fit around his neck or a weighty metal choke chain would simply fall over his ears and onto the ground when he put his head down.

The best solution is the so-called champagne safety collar, designed especially for the ex-racing Greyhound.

Safe Traveling

Traveling with a Greyhound is something many adopters enjoy, and it makes sense to be prepared for emergencies that may arise while away from home. It is good to have on hand a description of the type and dosage of anesthesia that should be used for a Greyhound, in the event you encounter a veterinarian unfamiliar with Greyhounds' anesthesia sensitivity. You can even handle some injuries that arise as you travel.

The American Red Cross and the Humane Society of the US have published *Pet First Aid,* available through the Red Cross, which also has a first-aid kit for sale. Or you can assemble your own kit, including hydrogen peroxide, cotton balls, antibiotic ointment, non-stick pads, gauze, tape, and "vet wrap."

It is made of strong, lightweight nylon webbing constructed in two connecting circles. By pulling up on the outer circle, which normally lies flat and has the ring that tags and a lead are attached to, the loop around the neck shortens to fit snugly, but not too tightly, right behind his ears. This collar is unlikely to slip over the Greyhound's head by accident, but it can also work like a choke collar, providing control without constriction. It can also work as a handle if you grasp the outer circle of the collar.

Special Care for Elderly Greyhounds

Before the Greyhound rescue and adoption movement became firmly established in the 1990s, ex-racers rarely lived much past the mandatory retirement age of five years. Dogs who didn't make it at the track (dogs who weren't earning money for their owners) were killed by the thousands, while some retired racers who might produce winning offspring were used for several years of breeding before meeting the same fate.

However, by the mid- to late 1990s, many hundreds of ex-racers reached ten years of age, and a Greyhound in his early teens was not unheard of. By the first few years of the 21st century, it appeared that estimates made years earlier that these dogs would live 12 to 14 years had, in fact, been accurate. Such a life expectancy is fairly unusual among large breed dogs, but given the chance to live as pets, Greyhounds thrived and grew old. One Greyhound, Suzi, adopted by Dick and Nancy Waddell of Ocean City, N.J., was 19 years old when she died in the spring of 2003.

A safety collar specially made for Greyhounds is probably the best to use for your pet. This design prevents the collar from slipping over the Greyhound's neck and head.

Aging, as humans know, is accompanied by new aches and pains, stiff joints, and more difficulty getting around and going up and down stairs. Greyhounds have similar problems as they age. Some of that soreness or lameness can be countered with daily supplements of glucosamine/chondroitin, which lubricates joints where cartilage has broken down.

"The interesting thing is older Greyhounds are a new breed because they were all destroyed prior to the adoption program," says Newman. "So now there's been a whole crop of older Greyhounds. We're getting a lot more information on these dogs as they hit 10, 11, 12 years of age, which they never did before."

The Adoption Community

The movement that revolves around saving ex-racing greyhounds is huge, spanning the country with rescue and adoption organizations in nearly every state. This movement spans the ideological spectrum, too. There are concerned and caring people inside the racing industry. There are national groups like Greyhound Pets of America that take a neutral stance on dog racing. There are local groups whose individual participants oppose racing but that have forged relationships with responsible track personnel to obtain dogs for adoption. And there are groups such as the Greyhound Protection League that oppose greyhound racing and monitor and publicize the horrors of the "sport" and GREY2KUSA, which was formed to try to put the dog racing industry out of business through legislation and ballot initiatives.

People involved in the Greyhound rescue and adoption movement come from virtually every strata of society and every corner of the country, creating a diverse community. Some people simply adopt a single Greyhound but do not become active in helping other retired racers find permanent homes. However, many, many others adopt one Greyhound and then another, and end up fostering Greyhounds, organizing fund-raising events, staffing outreach booths with their retired racers to spread the word about how sweet and companionable Greyhounds are, and visiting nursing homes and hospitals with their hounds.

Many people who have adopted retired racing Greyhounds attend the numerous Greyhound gatherings around the country.

There are also those who are unaffiliated with any particular adoption group but handle an important element in the chain of rescue, such as alerting others to an urgent need to move dogs from racetracks; arranging transportation for short and long distances; creating and selling Greyhound artwork and donating some or all of those proceeds to adoption efforts; or providing money to groups.

The Greyhound Project bridges the gap among groups. As an information source for anybody interested in Greyhound rescue and adoption, it publishes the quarterly *CG Magazine* and an annual Celebrating Greyhounds calendar featuring color and black-and-white photographs of retired racers. Adopters all over the country send in photographs of their retirees, hoping to have them appear in the calendar, which many rescue/adoption groups sell. In 1998, The Greyhound Project and the American Society for the Prevention of Cruelty to Animals launched an airport poster campaign in airports across the nation, using ad space that is unsold to publicize Greyhound adoption.

Greyhound Gatherings and Reunions

Greyhounds Reach the Beach—Dewey Beach, Delaware

In early October of the new millennium, Chloe, the Greyhound profiled in the Introduction of this book, was hanging around by the water in Dewey Beach, Delaware, with hundreds and hundreds of other retired athletes, including two of her younger siblings, Ruaidhri and Bonnie, and their cousins, Rodeo and Belle, all also adopted from the racetrack. Some of the Greyhounds were playing in the surf, others were digging holes with their play bows and showering everybody around them with sand, and some were just lounging around on the sand as if they were home in their living rooms on the couch. The people on the other ends of the hundreds of leashes were admiring each other's Greyhounds and exchanging information about where their dogs came from, how long they have had them, and how much they enjoy sharing their lives with these special dogs.

This scene has been repeated annually over the Columbus Day weekend since 1995, when plans by three couples to celebrate a wedding anniversary at the beach, accompanied by their Greyhounds, launched what has come to be the phenomenon known as Greyhounds Reach the Beach, which in 2002 was attended by 2,000 people and 3,000 Greyhounds.

The History

The Dewey Beach phenomenon really began with three couples: Pat and Wayne Tyson of Philadelphia, with retired racer Autumn; Judy and Mike Dillon of Denton, Maryland, with Chella; and Martha and Doug Sherman of West Chester, Pennsylvania, with Argus.

Greyhounds get a chance to play and bond with thousands of other retired racers at Greyhounds Reach the Beach, an annual event held in Dewey Beach, Delaware.

"It started by accident," says Joan Belle Isle, president of The Greyhound Project, which took over coordination of the wildly popular event in 1999.

The three women knew each other via a Greyhound news group on the Internet, finally meeting in person at a Greyhound picnic in Maryland in May 1995. Judy Dillon recalls that each of the three couples had adopted a Greyhound within the year and says, at the picnic, Pat Tyson talked about spending their wedding anniversary at the beach and taking their Greyhound. "I said I would like to do something like that someday," Dillon recalls, and soon the women were contacting motels along the seaboard to find one that would let them bring their Greyhounds.

An announcement that these couples were going to Dewey Beach with their dogs appeared on the then "very small Greyhound-List" e-mail group on the Internet, says Belle Isle. The Atlantic Oceanside was soon sold out, with participants coming from as far away as California and Canada, and the gathering totaled 75 people and about 50 Greyhounds. "It sort of blew everybody's socks off," Belle Isle recalls.

Dillon says as plans proceeded for the first Dewey Beach event, they kept adding names to the list of people who planned to attend and even decided to get stick-on nametags for everyone. Dillon says, "It started very small, and we didn't know what we were doing. We didn't know what people expected. We had no intention of making this any kind of event."

But it was an event, and they decided to try it again the following year. One hundred fifty people came the second year and 300 the third year. For the first five years, says Belle Isle, attendance doubled every year until "it got too big for three people to handle themselves." So The Greyhound Project, which provides information about and promotes the adoption of retired racing Greyhounds, and which has a corporate structure that could handle the increasingly complicated event, agreed to step in.

Belle Isle was the main speaker the second year, so she was familiar with Greyhounds Reach the Beach. And after her organization was approached, its board agreed to take on the burgeoning event.

"It was a little hard, but it was a relief, and I knew it was going to get better," says Dillon, who adds that the three founders still do some of the things they have done since the beginning, such as organizing the raffle, which at the suggestion of Martha Sherman, has benefited the Morris Animal Foundation since the second year and in 2002 provided over $9,000 to that foundation. They also continue to collect donations for the raffle and put together the attendee booklet.

In 2002, Greyhounds Reach the Beach was dedicated to "the three original Dewey dogs," Dillon says proudly. And although they were eight years older than at the first Dewey

---

Greyhound Heroes

CYNTHIA CASH

Cynthia Cash of Baton Rouge, Louisiana, is an independent adoption coordinator who has been the force behind many adoption hauls from racetracks and several rescues of ex-racers from medical research laboratories. After adopting her first retired racer in 1993, she worked with a local GPA chapter. Then, in 1995 she became involved in rescuing dogs from seasonal and permanent track closings and helped move 1,000 dogs out of peril the first year.

Her initial efforts were on behalf of Greyhounds at the low-grade Harlingen, Texas, and Juarez, Mexico, tracks where, she says, there "was no adoption option" and dogs had to be moved very quickly in order to save them. In addition to adoption groups, Cash enlisted help from the American Greyhound Council, the racing industry's animal welfare group. The tenacity she and others have shown over the years has paid off not just in the short term, when they mobilized to save dogs on short notice, but also in the long term, as some tracks that had once claimed they had no dogs available for adoption now have a kennel set aside for retired Greyhounds and sometimes even pay for transporting them to adoption groups.

Cash is widely credited with saving more than 200 Greyhounds on each of two occasions from Greenetrack in Alabama, which she says "was known as the largest kill track in the country... it was the end-of-the-line track in the United States... (and) had no adoptions ever." The track is now closed, probably forever. The first time she had help from the AGC, the second time from national animal charities.

Greyhounds Reach the Beach is the largest reunion for Greyhounds in the United States, an event that started as a small get-together for three couples and their Greyhounds.

event, Chella, Argus, and Autumn made the trip to see old friends and to make new ones.

Greyhounds Reach the Beach has spread out from the town of Dewey Beach to fill up Greyhound-friendly accommodations in neighboring communities, including Rehoboth Beach, Bethany Beach, and Lewes, and to become what Belle Isle calls a "whole area awash with Greyhounds for nearly a week in October."

"We don't care what people's (racing) politics are, provided they play well with others and leave their politics are home," she says.

Dewey Beach generates "a fair amount of media," Belle Isle says, with stories in major newspapers like *The Washington Post* and *The Philadelphia Inquirer*, which helps spread the word about retired racing Greyhounds.

"It's also been a really good way for people to network, remind themselves they actually do make a difference," says Bell Isle. "It's good for the soul for people who are in the trenches. You see all the dogs on the beach and see it does make a difference."

Greyhounds Reach the Beach is a combination street fair, continuing education course, shopping adventure, and just plain fun. From being predominantly a social occasion in its early years, Greyhounds Reach the Beach has expanded to include seminars on Greyhound health and welfare issues and speeches by people like Marion FitzGibbons and Betty White. FitzGibbons is president of the Irish Society for the

Greyhound Heroes

CLAUDIA PRESTO

Claudia Presto has taken an unusual journey in the rescue/adoption movement. She turned her life completely over to Greyhounds in the early 1990s, when she left a comfortable life in the New York corporate world and drove west in a pickup truck, pulling a camper trailer. She had been involved with Greyhounds since 1985, when she adopted Eliminator from a Connecticut racetrack and began spreading the word about the joys of retired racers through meet-and-greets. She left the East Coast the year after Eliminator's death, and she and her Greyhound, Slim, settled in Kanab, Utah, partly because it was near Best Friends no-kill animal sanctuary, where she worked for several months. Presto founded The Greyhound Gang in 1995, and the next year it became a nonprofit adoption group run out of her residence in the Utah desert. After a brief return to the corporate world to make the necessary money, she bought two and a half acres of sage, cactus, and red sand, fenced a quarter of an acre of it—for Greyhounds, of course–and moved into a 1,200-square-foot house on the property.

Her earliest efforts were picking up Greyhounds from the track in Tucson, Arizona, a ten-hour drive away, and bringing them back to her home for care that included spaying and neutering, love and attention, and social, emotional, and physical rehabilitation so the dogs could be adopted into permanent homes. But, she says, as a "one-person operation," she discovered she could only place about 20 to 40 dogs a year—as of 2003, she says, she had personally found homes for about 300 dogs—and decided, "I'm not going to save enough dogs this way."

Presto says two things changed her situation dramatically and enabled her to raise thousands and thousands of dollars for rescue and adoption efforts throughout the country. First, in 1999, a Greyhound adopter offered to do a new website for her for free and she started getting exposure; and secondly, she began selling a glucosamine powder to ease joint problems common in older retired racers.

Presto says she doesn't pay herself anything out of the money that she takes in through the Greyhound Gang, and has supplemented the cost of running it with a variety of endeavors that ranges from writing, entering contests (she won a home computer for having the most disorganized office), and cleaning houses, to the occasional foray back into the corporate world as a consultant.

Now that her emphasis has turned more toward raising funds to help Greyhound adoption, Presto gives out grants. In the first few years of the new millenium, she says she provided more than $30,000 in goods and money to other adoption groups "to help them do what they need to do." One group of beneficiaries in 2002 was 40 lucky Greyhounds in Florida who were to be euthanized because of broken legs. After being contacted by an adoption advocate there, Presto agreed to pay the veterinary bill, which came to $12,000, so the dogs could be saved and put up for adoption.

Prevention of Cruelty to Animals, and a tireless advocate for saving Irish Greyhounds from the horrors of track life, and death, in Spain. Actress Betty White is president emeritus and trustee of the Morris Animal Foundation, which is conducting a study of canine cancer for which The Greyhound Project has raised $100,000.

In a large tent, vendors of Greyhound-related items set up shop and are inundated with buyers. Some of the vendors are non-profit Greyhound rescue/adoption groups selling merchandise to fund their activities.

And there are also the somewhat less conventional events: a blessing of the hounds, held on the beach; a bonfire on the sand at which Greyhounds who have died—"crossed over the Rainbow Bridge" is how many adopters put it—are

In addition to conventional activities, Reach the Beach has featured unique events, such as a memorial bonfire and even a wedding ceremony in 2000, which included the couple's Greyhounds in the wedding party.

remembered; and in 2000, a marriage ceremony on the beach that included the couple's Greyhounds in the wedding party, was attended by strangers with their own Greyhounds, and ended with most of the canines in attendance joining in a celebratory, distinctive yodeling common to Greyhounds, "Roo! Roo! Roo!"

During Greyhounds Reach the Beach, Greyhounds are in the halls, elevators and lobbies of the dog-welcoming hotels and motels. Each day starts off with a walk on the sand at Dewey Beach for Greyhounds and their adopters, and all over the town of Dewey Beach, the sidewalks are busy from early morning to late night with strolling Greyhounds on leads held by their adopters.

"I still am overwhelmed," says Dillon. "When I walk over that sand dune on Saturday morning—I think last year (2002) is the first year I didn't cry. It just took my breath away to see all those dogs. It gave me goose bumps, and to think I had anything to do with it. That's the best part about being there: Just being there."

Greyhounds Reach the Beach is the largest but certainly not the only reunion of Greyhounds in the United States. Adoptions groups all over the country hold their own parties and picnics attended by Greyhounds they have helped to find permanent homes. Adopting an ex-racer opens a door to a rich and supportive social milieu, ranging from meet-and-greets at malls and stores to indoor and outdoor gatherings.

Greyhound Gathering—Kanab, Utah

Claudia Presto, founder of The Greyhound Gang, holds a Western US version of the Dewey Beach event in the tourist town of Kanab, Utah, in the spring. Called the Greyhound Gathering, it attracts Greyhound lovers from as far away as England and Canada and from 26 states.

THE HISTORY

"It all came about because I didn't have the money to go to Dewey Beach," Presto says. "And I wanted to be around all those Greyhounds. I wanted to see all those

Greyhound Gathering, held annually in the tourist town of Kanab, Utah, has attracted Greyhound lovers from 26 states, as well as Canada and England.

Greyhounds that were alive now because of people, because of adoption groups."

After some Greyhound-List chatter about how someone out West should do a "Dewey Beach"—and waiting for someone to step forward—Presto says she decided: "Okay, I'm having one. And it was basically because I wanted to have a party with Greyhounds."

In 1999, the first year, 125 people and about 150 dogs attended. The next two years, attendance was about double that. For 2003, the fifth Greyhound Gathering, 370 people and 400 dogs were registered, including two people from England and some Massachusetts Greyhound owners who have come every year, Presto says. She limits the number of participants "because I do this all on my own. It's my party and I'm throwing it, and I want to make sure everybody is having a good time, make sure everybody does everything with their dogs. In Dewey you can't bring your dogs a lot of places. Here, the only place you can't bring your dog is on the Best Friends (animal sanctuary) tour. But every place else, all the meals, all the activities, everything is about the dog being with you."

If the size and scale of the Greyhound Gathering are smaller than Dewey Beach, Presto still packs plenty of activities into the three days, including the Blur of Fur run; an elaborate costumed-Greyhound parade on Main Street of Kanab; the appearance of an Elvis impersonator who sings "You Ain't Nothin' But a Hound Dog;" and speakers on Greyhound health and welfare. And, of course, there is time for shopping and for adopters to exchange stories as they admire each other's Greyhounds. Participants can also visit some of the nation's most beautiful natural wonders at nearby Zion and Bryce Canyon National Parks and the Grand Canyon.

"Dewey Beach was absolutely my inspiration," Presto says. "And this has now taken on a life of its own."

Greyhound Planet Day: Making the World Safe for Greyhounds

A more recent addition to the register of Greyhound gatherings is Greyhound Planet Day: Making the World Safe for Greyhounds, which made its debut in September 2002 as the brain child of Therese Skinner of Kansas City, Missouri. Her impetus, she says, was a newspaper article a friend sent about a group of children in Lexington, Kentucky, who were raising money for a local Greyhound rescue group. "They do it every single year. I understand Greyhound groups get out here and do fund-raisers, but to have kids do it and for it to trickle through and come several states away, I thought it was so inspiring. I kept the article."

A short time later, another friend came to visit with her Greyhound, Rocky, whom she had recently adopted after he was rescued from a medical research laboratory to which a thousand Greyhounds had been illegally sold. "It touched me so much to know that at least one of those dogs got out of there safe and he's in a happy home," Skinner says. That was followed by the "buzz" on the Internet Greyhound-List about the thousands of retired racers that had been killed on an Alabama Greyhound farm, she says, and "I thought, we've got so much going on. If we could just set aside one day and devote it to the Greyhounds, here in the states, maybe it would trickle and have an effect. So I tossed the idea out there."

Greyhound Planet Day, a new addition to the gatherings for Greyhounds and their owners, was first conceived by Therese Skinner, pictured here.

Skinner says one of the people who responded from the Greyhound-List was Nancy Korman, who is involved in the American European Greyhound Alliance, formed to help save the Irish Greyhounds being exported to Spanish racetracks. Skinner says Korman told her Louise Coleman, a founder of AEGA, offered help on publicizing an event on a particular day.

"Well, I'm only one person," says Skinner. "Trying to get all the Greyhound groups throughout the United States all pulled together was not going to be feasible for me to do, so I jumped at the chance. Louise asked if we could make it not just nationwide but international. I thought, why not? We're going nationwide, so why not go full blast? The more we kept putting it out there, the more we kept getting a positive response. It just grew, and grew, and grew."

Greyhound groups in 30 states and eight countries participated, a turnout Skinner calls "just awesome." Individual groups fashioned their own activities, including walks, blessing of the hounds, selling microchip implants for identification, even bake sales. It was a day when the politics of racing were set aside, and groups with differing degrees of tolerance for the racing industry joined together to celebrate and promote Greyhounds. In addition to generating media attention in many places, Greyhound Planet raised money that went to local rescue groups and to AEGA. And plans were started almost immediately for a second annual Greyhound Planet Day.

Two weeks later, Skinner was at Dewey Beach, where "people were stopping me and thanking me" for Greyhound Planet. "I finally had to resort to taking my name tag off." Although Skinner is widely credited as the one who conceived Greyhound Planet Day, she attributes its success to the involvement of many other people. "An idea's only an idea, unless you have several people backing you up."

Not everyone can take off several days to travel across the country for a get-together like Greyhounds Reach the Beach or the Greyhound Gathering, but many adopters find a great measure of satisfaction in taking their Greyhounds to malls and pet-supply stores, where adoption groups set up booths that are part educational outreach and part social event; and to local festivals and fairs, where just walking around with a retired racer attracts attention and questions and gives the human a chance to show off—and to inspire someone else to adopt a retired racing Greyhound.

The Internet and Greyhound Adoption

The Internet has opened up a variety of resources for people interested and involved in adopting ex-racing Greyhounds. Many people in the rescue/adoption community are on the Greyhound-List, or Greyhound-L, as it is popularly known. It is an e-mailing list for sharing information on retired racers and welcomes anyone interested in the breed. Besides serving as a support resource for adopters, it helps with the placement of Greyhounds by acting as a networking tool for adoption/rescue groups. In 2003, there were more than 2,500 people around the country on the list. It has rules that must be observed and strongly discourages inflammatory or emotional rhetoric, but getting on it is easy— send an e-mail to LISTSERV@APPLE.EAST.LSOFT.COM and, in the text of the message, type "Subscribe Greyhound L" and your name.

Individual adoption groups often have their own e-mailing groups they use to keep local people up to date on events and incoming dogs from the racetracks.

The work of rescue and adoption groups has expanded in recent years to include finding homes for older dogs, often those used for breeding, and for dogs with injuries that ended their racing careers.

The Internet has also opened a myriad of fund-raising opportunities. Nonprofit groups no longer have to rely solely on local donations but can now make national appeals and raise money through raffles and auctions that are available online. If you have a computer and an Internet connection, there is no end to the information you can find. One website is the portal to several others, which in turn lead to more and a virtually limitless amount of help or information.

With all these groups and individuals working in so many ways to save the lives of thousands of ex-racing Greyhounds, it is no wonder that adoption is a Greyhound's best finish.

The Internet has opened up a variety of resources for people involved with the adoption of retired racing Greyhounds, providing support for adopters and aiding in the placement of Greyhounds by adoption/rescue groups.

About the Contributors

Claudia Presto

Claudia Presto's journey into the Greyhound rescue/adoption movement began in the early 1990s, when she left a comfortable life in the corporate world and headed west with a Chevy pickup truck, a camper trailer, and an retired racing Greyhound named Slim. In 1995, Presto founded The Greyhound Gang, and the next year it became a nonprofit adoption group run out of her residence in the Utah desert. Eventually, she expanded the adoption group to a larger plot of land, moved into a house on the property, and has been raising funds to help the adoption movement ever since. As of 2003, Presto has personally found homes for about 300 dogs.

Dr. Harry S. Newman, DVM

Harry S. Newman, DVM owner and founder of Georgetown Animal Clinic, attended the University of Buffalo and the New York State College of Veterinary Medicine at Cornell University. A Buffalo native, Dr. Newman served in the 431st Niagara Falls Air Force Medical Reserve unit as a veterinary officer. He has served terms as president of Niagara Frontier Veterinary Association, The Buffalo Academy of Veterinary Medicine, and The Buffalo Greyhound Adoption Society. In addition, Dr. Newman is one of the original founders of the Greater Buffalo Veterinary Emergency Clinic. He currently is a consultant for The Buffalo Greyhound Adoption Society as well as an active volunteer.

Dr. Sharon H. Smith, MD

Sharon H. Smith MD is a board certified Pediatric Hematologist/Oncologist in Indianapolis, Indiana, specializing in the care of children with brain tumors. She is a graduate of the University of Michigan and Indiana University School of Medicine. She adopted her first Greyhound in 1990 and has volunteered with a variety of organizations, including Michigan Greyhound Connection, Buffalo Greyhound Adoption, and USADOG. She is a founding board member of Greyhound Rescue Adoption Team in Buffalo, NY. She is active in all aspects of Greyhound rescue and competes in the sports of obedience and agility with her Greyhounds. In addition, her dogs are certified therapy dogs who visit children hospitals and nursing homes.

Nancy Hudson

Nancy Hudson is Vice President and Training Director of TLC Greyhound Adoption/GPA Kansas. She has been training, showing, and breeding dogs since she was a teenager and is past President and Training Director of the Hutchinson, Kansas Kennel Club. For the past three years, she has been managing the Greyhound adoption program at the Hutchinson Correctional Facility and teaches weekly training classes for the inmate handlers and their foster Greyhounds. She resides near Hutchinson, Kansas with seven retired racing Greyhounds.

Maggie McCurry

Maggie McCurry has been a pilot for over 17 years. In 1996, she decided to combine her love of flying with her compassion for animals and began to fly retired racing Greyhounds from the rescue centers at the racetracks to outlying adoption groups who could place them in loving homes. McCurry has since flown hundreds of retired racing dogs to safety. Wings for Greyhounds has been featured in many television shows and news stories over the years, and it is McCurry's hope that the publicity generated by this unique airborne rescue project will help to promote Greyhounds as companion animals and increase the number of adoptions.

Cynthia C. Cash

Living in Baton Rouge, Louisiana with a pack of adopted animals, Cynthia C. Cash heads her own practice as a landscape architect and is an adjunct professor in the same field at Louisiana State University. An avowed animal lover since childhood, she devotes a great deal of energy toward improving options for surplus Greyhounds once their racing days are over. Her focus has been on the long-distance transfer of hounds, either from track closings or the day-to-day necessity of moving them out of Florida (home to one-third of all racing dogs). She has also been instrumental in obtaining the release of ill-begotten Greyhounds from beings subjects in medical research facilities. In addition, she spearheaded the national Adopt-A-Greyhound airport ad campaign, sponsored by The Greyhound Project, the ASPCA, and Petsmart Charities. At the local level, she volunteers with the Louisiana chapter of the Greyhound Pets of America (GPA).

Joan Belle Isle

Joan Belle Isle's adoption of her Greyhound, Proud Truth, known to his friends as King Tut, launched her on the journey into the Greyhound rescue and adoption movement. Starting as an occasional volunteer, she eventually became a board member with a local Greyhound adoption organization. In 1993, along with several other Greyhound adopters, she was among the founders of The Greyhound Project. For the past ten years, the Project has focused on supporting Greyhound adopters and promoting Greyhound adoption across the country. Some of their activities include the Adoption Resource Directory, the Adopt A Greyhound airport advertising campaign, the Celebrating Greyhounds calendars and magazine, the annual Greyhound Reach the Beach gathering at Dewey Beach, and the Greyhound Cancer Research Fund at the Morris Animal Foundation.

Kelly Graham

Kelly Graham founded Golden Years Senior Greyhounds after learning about the large number of senior dogs living out their retirement years on breeding farms because their owners didn't realize anyone would want them. GYSG began as a referral program with a strong Internet presence but soon grew into a placement program, finding homes for scores of elderly Greyhounds. Graham balances her passion for senior dogs with a career in technical communication with a world leader in automation. She shares her Ohio home with a dozen Greyhounds, two Italian Greyhounds, and five Chihuahuas.

Therese Skinner

Therese Skinner lives in Kansas City, Missouri with her husband, Toby and their three Greyhounds: Jackie, Heisman, and Ashley, fondly known as the Gentle Hugs Greyhounds. She promotes Greyhound adoption through Heisman's Greyhound Art store and other various fundraisers. Skinner has been active in animal adoption for 40 years and works diligently all year long on Greyhound Planet Day to make the world safer for Greyhounds.

Index

Index

Photo Credits

Carolyn Raeke, 5, 11, 63, 67, 75, 79, 81, 83, 87, 91

Sue LeMieux, 6, 7, 12, 13, 17, 19, 23, 24, 29, 32, 43, 47, 48, 55, 61, 70, 73, 77

Steve Surfman, 8

Jini Foster, 28, 39, 88

Julie Williams, 31

Isabelle Francais, 34

Brad Wood, 34, 44, 56

Heather Minnich, 119

Therese Skinner, 89

Mark Scioto, 62

Other photos: Joseph Chambers, Aileen Desiata, Isabelle Francais, Robert Pearcy, and Ron Reagan.

Resources

ORGANIZATIONS

American Greyhound Council
C/o The National Greyhound Association
P.O. Box 543
Abilene, KS 67410-0543
(785) 263-4660
www.agcouncil.com

American Kennel Club
260 Madison Avenue
New York, NY 10016
Phone: (212) 696-8200
Or 5580 Centerview Drive
Raleigh, NC 27606
Phone: (919) 233-9767
www.akc.org

Greyhounds in Need (UK)
5 Greenways
Egham, Surrey TW20 9PA
Phone: 00 44 1784 436845
Fax: 00 44 1784 477490
E-mail: anne@greyhoundsinneed.com
www.greyhoundsinneed.co.uk

Greyhound Pets of America
(800) 366-1472
E-mail: greyhoundpets@
greyhoundpets.org
www.greyhoundpets.org

Greyhound Protection League
GPL National Office
P. O. Box 669
Penn Valley, CA 95946
(800) 4-HOUNDS or (800) 446-8637
www.greyhounds.org

Greyhound Rescue (UK)
Castledon Kennels
181 Castledon Road
Wickford, Essex SS12 OEG
Phone: 01268 733293
www.dog-rescue.org.uk/greyhound.htm

National Greyhound Adoption Program
4701 Bath Street
Philadelphia, PA 19137
(800) 348-2517 or (215) 331-7918
Fax: (215) 331-1947
E-mail: ngap@ix.netcom.com
www.ngap.org

The Greyhound Gang
C/o Claudia Presto
P.O. Box 274
Kanab, UT 84741
(435) 644-2903
E-mail: Claudia@greyhoundgang.com
www.greyhoundgang.org

The Greyhound Project, Inc.
P.O. Box 358
Marblehead, MA 01945
www.adopt-a-greyhound.org

The Retired Greyhound Trust (UK)
149a Central Road
Worcester Park, Surrey KT4 8DT
Phone: 0870 444 0673
Fax: 0870 908 2525
E-mail: greyhounds@retiredgreyhounds.co.uk
www.retiredgreyhounds.co.uk

Wings for Greyhounds, Inc.
P.O. Box 21065
Sedona, AZ 86341-1065
(888) 4WE-FLYM
E-mail: weflym@aol.com
www.wingsforgreyhounds.org

MAGAZINES

Celebrating Greyhounds magazine
C/o The Greyhound Project, Inc.
P.O. Box 358
Marblehead, MA 01945
www.adopt-a-greyhound.org/
cgmagazine/subscribe.html

Greyhounds
Fancy Publications, Inc.
3 Burroughs
Irvine, CA 92618
Phone: (888) 738-2665
Fax: (949) 855-3045
www.fancypubs.com

EMERGENCY SERVICES

Animal Poison Hotline
(888) 232-8870

ASPCA Animal Poison Control Center
(888) 426-4435
www.aspca.org